CONTENTS

CONTENTS

MY DADDY
THE PEDOPHILE

PROLOGUE

When I was little, Daddy and I played pretend games. The first pretend game I can remember playing was the Lollipop Game when I was four years old. This was a game we played only when no one else was home. In the bathroom Daddy would have me pretend his private part was a lollipop, and I was to lick it like I was enjoying the biggest, sweetest-tasting lollipop ever. If I pretended really well, Daddy would get me a real lollipop to enjoy. Sometimes we would hear the front door open, and quickly the game would end. "Shh, remember, Lil, this is our game, our secret," Daddy would whisper, and out of the bathroom we'd go, our game over until next time.

Sometimes I would tell Daddy I did not want to play. Like when it was just Daddy and me in his pretty blue Chevy station wagon, and he would say in his strange, sexy voice, "Come here, Lil."

Knowing what would happen when I heard that voice, I would angrily respond, "No! I don't want to!"

He would reply soothingly, "Oh, Lily, come on now. You know this is just how daddies show that they love their special daughters. So, come here, come on." Not really wanting to, I would slowly move toward him as he gently guided me over the shiny blue bench seat and pulled me onto his lap. "Remember, Lil, no one else in the whole wide

3

world will ever love you more than your Daddy," Daddy would say as he reached between my legs. I would gaze out the window and pretend I was anywhere but there.

I would always feel happiest when Daddy's games were over— when it was finally my turn to choose the next game Daddy and I would play.

Chapter 1
RUNNING AWAY

I was standing at the top of the stairs hoping I had everything I needed when I looked down and saw my pregnant mom hovering at the bottom of the staircase. She was waiting impatiently for me to come down, puffing wildly on a Pall Mall cigarette, white smoke filling the air. Mom was angry with me. Again. Usually her anger left me paralyzed, frozen with fear and unable to run, but not tonight. Not this time. Tonight, I would run away, and shockingly, my mom would let me go.

As I stood there, she glared up at me and our eyes locked. She gave me her death stare, which always left me trembling with fear. *Well, whatever the future holds in store for me,* I thought, *has to be better than this.* Panic swept through me, and my heart began beating like crazy as I made my way down the stairs. But I knew everything would be fine as soon as I left. It had to be.

In the hallway, Mom stood inches from my face. Her big brown eyes narrowed to hostile slits and turned cold, piercing right through me. But I stood my ground and stared right back. We were engaging in a fierce unblinking battle of wills which I was determined to win when suddenly, without warning, she snatched my purse from my hand and emptied the contents onto the table. She inspected each item, searching for my stash of drugs. She came up with nothing, because the speed she sought I had tucked safely in my bra inside a small plastic baggie. I held my breath and prayed a pat-down search would not follow. Angry and frustrated, Mom threw the items back into my purse and flung it at me. "So, you hate living here, do you? Think you'd be happier living somewhere else?" I nodded. "Well, mark my words, Lily—you'll end up in a gutter someplace, hungry, cold and penniless!" She handed me a carton of Marlboros. "Don't say your mother never gave you anything!" She laughed. "You've got twenty-four hours before I call the cops. And if they pick you up, I won't come to get you like I did last time. This time you're on your own. This time you can rot in juvenile hall for all I care."

Yeah, well, this time, I thought to myself, *I'm* not *going to get caught.*

She shoved me toward the door and said, "Now, get out!" I was only too happy to oblige.

Earlier Mom had allowed me to take only what I could wear, so I chose carefully. I wore my favorite pair of Palmetto jeans, a shiny pink silk blouse with long sleeves over a plain white t-shirt, and of course, my black down jacket for when it got cold. I couldn't leave my beautiful, iridescent abalone shell necklace behind, so I put it around my neck.

In the bathroom I gathered all the bathroom necessities and stuffed them in my purse, make-up included. I gazed at myself in the mirror. I was five feet six inches tall, one hundred and twenty pounds, with bright hazel eyes, auburn hair, and a nearly perfect 36(D)-26-34 hourglass figure. Many guys said I looked like I'd just stepped off a page from *Playboy.* Everywhere I went I was noticed, even when I didn't want to be. But despite all the attention I attracted, I still felt empty and alone. I thought no one could ever truly love me because I was too broken, too messed up.

Turning off the bathroom light, I walked back into my room. I said goodbye to my closet full of clothes and my belongings: my jewelry, posters, stuffed animals, record albums, yearbooks, knickknacks, photos—all my stuff that held special memories for me. But I was glad to leave all the bad memories behind.

A few months earlier, Mom's latest man, Ned, had moved in with us. He was much younger than she, tall and thin, an auto mechanic and Vietnam veteran. He shared scary, surreal stories about the war and how after he got back home he had turned to drugs such as marijuana to survive and escape the horrors he had witnessed.

I hated Ned. Recently, when my mom had gone snooping through my room and found my stash of speed and marijuana, Ned became irate with me. Finding me alone in the tiny kitchen, he shouted, "How dare you have drugs and not share them with me! If you ever do that again, I'll plant drugs in your room, call the cops, and have you sent away for a very long time! So don't you *ever*—" Suddenly, my mom entered the kitchen as Ned continued, "I repeat, don't you *ever* let me catch you doing drugs again, you hear?" As I stood there shocked and speechless, I realized Ned was a deceitful, despicable man. I loathed and distrusted him, but at least he hadn't snuck into my bedroom at night like the one before him.

Mom and Ned's plan was to sell everything they owned, hit the road in his truck camper, and start a new family in Idaho. My siblings, eleven-year-old Eileen and five-year-old Bart, wanted to go. I was sixteen and had no intention of moving anywhere.

It was a cold January night in 1977 when I ran away from my mom for the last time. As I turned the corner, relieved that I wouldn't be leaving California and heading to Idaho with Mom and Ned, I realized I had no money and nowhere to go. *Now what?* I wondered. I had only twenty-four hours to figure out a plan before the cops might come for me, and that was if my mom kept her word and waited the twenty-four hours to report me. The thought of being locked away until I was eighteen terrified me. I called my boyfriend

Vance. He told me not to worry, just come over. I couldn't get there fast enough.

Vance's parents were less than thrilled with their twenty-six-year-old son and his underage girlfriend living together. They were nervous about possible legal issues—like statutory rape—and felt a more sensible solution would be for me to move in with them. They wanted to care for me. So after three weeks of living at Vance's, I moved in with his parents, and they contacted an attorney to begin the process of becoming my legal guardians.

The following week their attorney, Mr. Silva, phoned me to ask some routine questions which I didn't mind answering. But when he asked me "Father's name," I felt a strange sense of déjà vu as I remembered the night a cranky old lady at Santa Cruz Juvenile Hall asked me the same question four years before. That morning I'd ditched my school books, grabbed my stuff—a canteen of Kool-Aid, a small bottle of Johnson's Baby Shampoo, a few packs of Marlboros, two dollars and fifty-six cents, and some make-up—and hitchhiked thirty miles south down the coast to the Santa Cruz Beach Boardwalk with my girlfriend. There, without a flutter of hesitation, we threw off our shoes and ran into the waves, splashing, giggling, and feeling so carefree, we wished the moment would never end. But that night under the Boardwalk, we were busted and thrown into juvenile hall for running away from home.

"Father's name," the older gray-haired lady sitting behind her typewriter had asked me, raising her brow and waiting for my reply.

"Which one?" I asked.

"Well, how many are there?" she asked, staring at me with a half puzzled, half annoyed look.

"Three."

"Okay, how 'bout we go with the first one," she said, irritated.

"Okay, Bill Capello," I replied.

"Father's address," the monotone voice asked.

"I don't know. I haven't seen him since I was seven," I replied. Mom and Dad had divorced when I was two but shared custody of me until I was seven. At that point, in Santa Cruz Juvenile Hall, I hadn't seen him in five years.

"Okay, how about your second father then," she barked. I wondered why she seemed to be in such a hurry.

"Jeffrey Styles," I responded.

"His address," she snapped as her fingers rested impatiently above the typewriter keys, eager to type my response.

"Somewhere in London, England," I replied. Mom and Jeffrey, a kind, soft-spoken Englishman, had married when I was six and divorced when I was ten. I hadn't seen him since he had returned home to London the month before.

"Okay, then, how 'bout your third father," she said, frustrated, shaking her head and rolling her eyes.

"Sure, Carlos Sanchez," I said. My latest father and Mom's own first cousin—electrician by day, child molester by night—was an arrogant, cruel man who had started molesting me the year before. I hated him; he was part of the reason I'd run away.

Now, four years later, I had to go through the questioning again over the phone.

"Sorry, I didn't hear you, Lily. What did you say your father's name was?" Mr. Silva asked me again. *Great*, I thought, *here we go again*.

"Which one?" I asked.

"Well, how many are there?" he asked.

"Three, or maybe four, I'm not sure," I said, wondering if Mom and Ned had married.

"Hmm ... Well, let's start with the first one," Mr. Silva said.

"Okay, his name's Bill Capello," I said.

"Bill Capello, you say? By any chance is he a private investigator?" he asked, surprised.

"What? I don't know. I haven't seen him since I was seven," I said.

"Okay, do you remember anything about him?"

"Well...he used to live in Campbell. He had a wife named Betsy, or something like that. And I remember playing with Rick, my older brother. There was a baby too, but I don't remember his name." I couldn't really remember what my dad looked like anymore. It had been nine years since I had seen him, and my mom had destroyed all his photos, so my memories were hazy at best.

"Okay—I think I may know your father. Let's put this process on hold while I try to locate him. If I do locate him, would you like to speak with him?"

I hesitated. "Yeah, I guess." I wasn't sure how I felt about my father. Sometimes I missed him, but I didn't like to think about it because when I did, it hurt far too much. Since he had never tried to contact me, I assumed he didn't care about me. I doubted he'd even want to speak to me. I hung up the phone feeling anxious and a little numb.

A few days later, Vance's petite mother, Pat, called me over to chat. "Lily, Mr. Silva called. He's located your father. It just so happens your father is a private investigator who works for Mr. Silva. He spoke with your father, who said he'd like to meet with you if that's okay. Would you like that?"

"Gee, Pat, I don't know. I'm kind of nervous," I said.

"Why?" she asked.

"Well, I don't really know him. The last time I saw him, I was seven. My mom said that my father was a terrible man but never explained why. What if he is?" I asked. I had no bad memories of my father, but it seemed like my mom did.

"I've found when people go through a divorce, emotions run high, and sadly, it's very common for many mean and hurtful things to be said in the heat of the moment. I wouldn't worry too much about your mother's comments regarding your father," Pat said.

"Really?" I asked.

"Yes," she said, nodding. "We can have your father come by the house and see how it goes. You don't have to do anything you don't want to. Remember, you're always welcome to stay here. That hasn't changed."

"Okay, thanks," I said.

"You're welcome," she said and gave me a reassuring hug.

The next day, as the three o'clock meeting time drew near, I felt nervous and paced the floor, my eyes darting between the clock and the front window. I wondered if my biological father and I had ever crossed paths before and I didn't even know it. After Jeffrey had adopted me, my mom insisted that he was my "real" and only father, and there would be no more talk about Bill ever again; it was like he never existed. And yet he did exist because I was about to meet him.

Chapter 2
REUNITED

As I anxiously waited to meet my father, I remembered how when I was little I'd get so excited counting down the days until Saturday, when I'd get to see him again. It seemed like forever until he came by Mom's house and picked me up for my weekend visitations. Staring out the window waiting for him, I'd imagine all the fun things we would do together. There were trips to the movies, slot car tracks, and petting zoos. To make me laugh, he would do things like tell me silly jokes, play horsie, or tickle me until I begged him to stop. One of my favorite things he did was pull quarters out from behind my ears. I could never forget how he could always make me laugh.

I watched the clock tick closer to three o'clock and thought back to nine years earlier when my father had given me up for adoption to Jeffrey. My father told me that he wouldn't be able to come and pick me up anymore for weekend visits because I had a new family now and I needed to live there with them. Suddenly all visitations with my father stopped. I was devastated. My seven-year-old mind reasoned that for my father to stop seeing me I must be the most horrible child who had ever lived. I hated myself for whatever I had done wrong. It hurt so badly inside that I didn't even want to live anymore. I couldn't imagine life without my father. He was supposed to love and protect me, not leave me.

The last time I saw my father was when he visited me in the hospital, less than a month after he'd stopped visitations. I had undergone surgery because my appendix had burst. I had jaundice, peritonitis, and the very serious life-threatening condition called septicemia, or blood poisoning. The doctors didn't think I would make it, and while I dreamt of dying only to awaken in Angel Land, a secret place I knew of where only angels dwell in a bright white and pink glow, and I could run my little fingers through their silky soft white wings, I didn't think I would make it either.

I will never forget the last conversation my father and I had, when I lay dying in my hospital bed. "Lil, I need you to promise me something—and it's *very, very* important," my father said seriously.

"Okay, Daddy, *anything*," I eagerly replied.

"I need you to promise me that you'll be the brave Lil I know that you are, and go in there," my father said, pointing at my stomach, "and fight all those bad, bad guys that are making you sick. Can you do that for your daddy?"

I nodded.

"And if you should ever need me when you're in there fighting, just picture your daddy, and I'll be right there, fighting right alongside you. I promise. Okay, Lil?" my father said, gently squeezing my hand.

I nodded again, still holding my father's hand.

"You know, those bad guys don't stand a chance!" My father smiled knowingly.

I smiled back knowingly too.

"And if you should get scared while you're fighting those bad guys, I want you to hug this little guy right here, okay?" my father said as he pointed at Pinkie, a six-foot-long, rainbow-colored stuffed snake with black stripes he had given me that day. "Just wrap him around you, and he'll hug you right back." I placed my skinny little hand, trailing an IV tube, on Pinkie's head and petted him.

"I love you, Lil," he said, smiling. A tear fell softly on my father's cheek. "Now go and be my brave little girl." My father leaned over, gave me a hug, and kissed me on my forehead.

"Okay, Daddy, I will. I promise. I love you too." As he turned to leave, I asked, "Will I ever see you again, Daddy?"

He smiled. "Yes, you will Lil, one day."

"Do you promise, Daddy?" I asked, starting to cry.

"Yes, I promise. But until that day comes, I want you to hold on to Pinkie really, really tight, and remember that your daddy loves you very, very much, okay, Lil?"

"Okay, Daddy."

I fell back asleep and dreamt of going to battle. I had to. I'd given my word to my father, and I always kept my promises, no matter what. My father knew that, and so did I. So I fought. And on those days when I felt like I was losing the battle, I pictured my father, who somehow appeared right next to me, just as he'd said he would.

A month later, I was released from the hospital. My doctor said I was a lucky girl to be alive. I knew I was lucky and alive because I had a father who loved me. My father had saved my life. He was the only one who could have. We'd had a special bond and love like no other.

But that was a long time ago, and over the years I had slowly forgotten him. That day in the hospital seemed like another lifetime in another world.

Suddenly, the doorbell rang. I stood frozen and looked over at Pat. She smiled, put her arm around my shoulder, walked with me to the door, and opened it. In stepped my father. He looked nothing like I had pictured or even vaguely remembered. He was around five feet eight inches tall, of average build with black hair, a mustache, a rather large nose, and brown eyes. My first impression of him was not favorable—he reminded me of a weasel—and I wasn't finding any sort of resemblance between us. *Great*, I thought. Pat led us to the living room to sit, offered us something to drink, and then left us to converse uninterrupted.

"Do you remember much about me?" my father asked.

"No, not really," I replied, feeling nervous. I thought I had remembered a lot about my father, but this man sitting across from me didn't look familiar at all.

"Well, let me start off by telling you a little bit about myself, so that I don't seem like such a stranger to you. My name is William, but people who know me just call me Bill. I'm a private investigator, or PI—"

"You mean like that guy on TV, Baretta, who always says, 'Don't do the crime if you can't do the time'?" I asked.

"Sort of, Lily, but Baretta's a police detective, and I'm a private detective, more like Rockford from *The Rockford Files*." He smiled, and I nodded and smiled back as I started to relax. I didn't care which TV detective he was more like. My father was a real-life detective, and I thought that was pretty darn cool.

"I live across town near the foothills with my second wife Betty and our two children, Connor and Chrissy. They'd really like to meet you," he said. He paused, then continued. "I'd really like to get to know my daughter better. Do you mind if I ask you a few questions?"

"No, I guess not," I said.

My father began to ask me basic questions about my favorite food, favorite subject in school, even my favorite color.

We chatted for a while, and then his face turned serious. "Lily, why'd you run away?"

"Mom was moving to Idaho, and I didn't want to go," I said. That was as much as I felt comfortable telling this man who happened to be my father but who felt more like a stranger.

There was a short silence, and then he asked, "Want to know a somewhat unusual fact or two about me?"

"Sure," I said. He suddenly had my full attention.

"I was a preemie born on April Fool's Day. I weighed less than three pounds. Can you believe I was so small that I went home in a shoebox?" my father asked.

"No way!" I said, amazed.

"Way!" he chuckled, then continued. "Do you know how I met your mom?"

I shook my head. "No, I don't."

"I met your mom in the summer of '59. I was twenty-one, and she was sixteen. The funny thing is I met her while she was dating my best friend. She found my buddy very boring, but found me far more interesting. She broke up with my friend and immediately started dating me. She said my buddy held her hand like it was a dead fish, but when I held her hand, well, she felt sparks. She also liked my sense of humor. I could always make her laugh." He smiled. I smiled back, remembering how he could always make me laugh, too.

"What did you like about my mom?" I asked.

"Well, she was smart, outgoing, and funny. Her long thick hair, big brown eyes, and perfect hourglass shape made her look like some kind of movie star. She was the most beautiful girl I'd ever seen," he said, "and I felt like the luckiest guy in the world to be with her. We dated, fell in love, and got married two months later." All my life, I'd heard how beautiful my mother was. People were completely blinded by her beauty, but I wasn't. When I looked at her, all I could see was the ugliness inside her. I wondered if my father had ever seen that ugliness too.

"Why'd you marry so young?"

"Your mom wanted to escape her abusive home. Her alcoholic father had molested her, and her mother had beaten her," he explained. I was shocked but fascinated to hear these family stories for the first time. My mom had never talked about her past. "I felt terrible for your mom," my father said as he looked down at the floor. "I wanted to help her out of her bad situation."

As we sat there, I noticed the strangest thing: the more my father and I talked, the more I became comfortable in his presence, and the more his weasel image faded into a sweeter, cuter otter image. His sense of humor and charm seemed to magically airbrush his rough edges away.

"Lily, is there anything you'd like to ask me?"

I thought for a moment. "Yes, why did you divorce my mom?"

"Well, I never wanted to divorce your mom. I loved her, and you, very much. I wanted to be married to her forever. But your mom left me. She was very unhappy," he said with tears in his eyes.

"But, if you loved me so much, then why haven't I seen you since I was seven?" I had never understood why.

"You know, I never wanted to give you up," he said, "but I did because I didn't want to fight your mom for custody and drag you through the courts. So I let you go. It was the hardest thing I've ever done in my life. Not a day has gone by that I haven't thought about you. I've missed you so much. I hoped and prayed that one day, when you got older, you would want to find your father. I'm so happy to have this chance to see you again. You're my daughter and I love you very much."

I was touched. There was nothing I had ever wanted more than to have a parent who loved me. I'd never felt my mom loved me. Sometimes I doubted she even liked me. Many times she would rather hit me than listen to me. It felt like she didn't even see who I was.

I'll never forget one rainy day when I stood on the sidewalk staring down at six or seven skinny, pale-brown worms wiggling in a deep puddle on my way to school, wondering what I should do. My second grade classmate told me that if worms were in water over their heads they'd drown, but my mom told me that if I were late for school one more time I'd be punished. I wanted to walk away, but I couldn't. Instead, I gently picked up each worm and carefully placed each one on safer drier ground, promising them that everything would be okay.

When I got home that day, my mom cornered me in the backyard where I had gone to play. "Lily! What did I tell you about going straight to school? Get over here right now!" Nothing was scarier than my mom when she was mad. I prepared for battle, a battle I could never win. I was brought into the ring. Angry, unstoppable Mom was the bull, scraping the ground with her hoof, head down, ready to charge, and I was the bright red cloth that hung from a stick.

"How dare you not listen to your mother!" she screamed. Then she hit me hard across the face. "Are you going to be late for school again, Lily? Well? Well? Answer me when I'm talking to you!"

"No...o." I tried to get the words out, trembling as I stared right into the eyes of my mom, the eyes of a wild, raging bull.

A hard blow across my backside sent me flying to the ground; the cool damp grass felt soothing against my still burning, slapped cheek. I looked up and saw my mom standing over me yelling, "What the hell's wrong with you, not doing what you're told! Well? You don't know how to listen? Are you stupid?" Her words and strikes burned me as if I were placing my body on a hot stove.

The next thing I knew my mom grabbed me by my hair, yanked me off the ground, and hit me some more. Her face was in mine, and she was yelling loudly. I kept turning away, but Mom kept forcing my head back to look at her. After she got tired of hitting me, she stormed off cursing and left me standing there in tears, sore all over, warm blood dripping from my nose. There were many abusive scenes just like this one permanently etched in my memory.

As I looked at my dad, I realized how strange it felt to not be afraid, to not want to run. "Would you like to go and meet your siblings?" Dad asked as he got up from the chair.

"Okay," I said. I wasn't sure if I was more anxious or excited.

The drive to my dad's house on Minx Drive in San Jose took about twenty minutes, but it felt like hours. As I sat next to him, my stomach knotted into a tight ball. I didn't want my dad to know that I was still a little uneasy around him and nervous to meet my siblings and stepmother. I kept smiling and telling myself they weren't strangers; they were my family, so I had nothing to worry about.

Dad pulled into the driveway, which led up to a nice two-story home painted in white and trimmed in brick with a basketball hoop above the two-car garage. The front yard had a well-maintained lawn and a clump of three weeping birches on the left. I followed Dad up the path to the house. On the porch a few pots full of colorful flowers and a brown doormat that said *Welcome* put me at ease.

Inside I met my siblings, a family friend, and my dad's wife. First, I greeted my sister Chrissy, a pretty six-year-old girl in a light blue dress with long, straight blonde hair parted down the middle. She blushed and gave me a shy smile, and I smiled back. I could tell she was nervous about meeting her new big sister for the first time. She sat down on the couch and watched me. Next I was introduced to my brother Connor, a short and stocky eleven-year-old with dark wavy hair and brown eyes. I had met Connor before when he was a baby. He flashed me a dazzling smile as we shook hands. Then I met Eric, a blond-haired, blue-eyed, sixteen-year-old like me. Dad's friend Eric came from a broken and unhappy home. He spent a great deal of time at my dad's house, like a member of the family. Finally, I met my dad's second wife of nearly fourteen years, Betty. Betty was much older than my mom; she was forty-five and my mom was thirty-three. Her short haircut seemed to draw attention to her intense dark eyes. I was aware I had known her before when I was young, but couldn't recall very much about her except she liked cats. In the garage I met the latest litter. Chrissy showed me her favorite kitten with pretty pale blue eyes like hers, cuddled in a loving heap of five inside a box. Behind the box was Connor's pride and joy: a silver metallic 1973 Honda CR125M Elsinore. Connor stared lovingly at the bike as if it were a living, breathing thing. His face lit up as he explained dirt bike riding to me. He liked the rush he felt as he dug into the turns or soared high in the air. In the backyard I met Connor's beloved dog Buddy, a shaded sable Sheltie. I knelt down and Buddy jumped up and licked my face. I laughed, relaxing a little more.

We sat in the living room and chatted for a while. I found out that Betty and Dad had been foster parents for years, and Dad was very involved in his local Catholic church and its Knights of Columbus organization. Dad was diabetic, needing daily insulin injections to control his blood sugar. Betty was a stay-at-home mom. She had recently started working part time at Newberry's, a nearby five-and-dime store.

Before dinner, Connor brought out an extra chair for me while Chrissy set the table. I thought it was sweet that Connor and Chrissy both wanted to sit next to me, so to please them both I sat between them and ate my first dinner with my new family. Betty served a pot roast and heated herself up a Weight Watchers dinner. She told me she was on a diet and had recently lost a lot of weight but still wanted to lose ten pounds more. I stared at her and couldn't understand why. I thought she looked pretty good and was already quite thin, but I nodded anyway. Betty and Dad did a good job of keeping the conversation flowing and warding off any lulls, which made me feel more comfortable during the awkwardness of eating dinner with strangers who happened to be my family.

After dinner my twenty-one-year-old brother Rick came by for a visit. Rick was a son from a previous marriage between Betty and my dad's older brother. Dad had adopted Rick when he married Betty. I didn't remember much about him, just flashes of us teasing, arguing, laughing, and playing together. Of course he was all grown up now with a stocky build and a gorgeous smile like Connor's. He had married his high school sweetheart and they now had a baby girl. They lived close by in the foothills. He gave me a big hug and said he still remembered me. He had wondered from time to time where I was and how I was doing. It felt good to know he had missed me, even though I hadn't thought much about him until then.

Dad pulled out some photo albums and laid them on the table. Everyone was eager to share holiday photos, vacation photos, school photos, and baby photos of Rick, Connor, Chrissy, and me. *Me*. I had never seen baby photos or any photo of me before the age of four. My mom had cut up that whole part of my past.

Here, my pictures were kept safe and tucked away in photo albums. I flipped through a well-worn black photo album and paused to study pictures of me. I looked so happy. One photo caught my eye, and the more I looked at it, the more alive it became. Dad had taken Rick and me to Disneyland when I was five. I could almost hear my squeals of delight as I ran like lightning toward the Palomino Belgian horse standing as still as a statue in front of Sleeping Beauty's Castle. I could almost feel his velvet soft nose and whiskers. I had loved the way his warm breath felt on my little hands, and in that magical moment I'd felt like I knew him and he knew me.

Chrissy understood as she looked at the Disney horse photo with me. She felt a deep connection with horses too. She offered me her favorite dark brown Breyer stallion model horse to hold, which I accepted. She smiled, thrilled to have a new big sister who loved horses like she did.

Betty and Dad asked me to stay the night, reminding me that I was family and was welcome to stay as long as I wanted. In bed that night I lay awake thinking. It was a lot to take in—a new home, a new family. I could still feel the knot in my stomach, but it was a lot smaller. *Could I really be happy here?* I wondered. I did feel welcome. Somehow I even felt like I belonged here, but I still wasn't one hundred percent sure if I wanted to stay.

Chapter 3
RECONNECTING

The next morning Dad and I sat on the barstools in the kitchen drinking coffee and talking. We had a lot of catching up to do. "Did you know that when I came home from the hospital, I slept with that stuffed snake Pinkie every night?" I said, smiling. Dad smiled back. "Don't laugh, okay? But the tighter I held onto him, the happier I felt."

"And why's that?" Dad asked.

"Cuz, I knew that wherever you were, you still loved me, just like you did when you came to visit me in the hospital that day," I said.

"Yes, I've always loved you," Dad said, hugging me.

"Can you believe Mom threw Pinkie away when I was ten? I was so sad, I cried for weeks."

"Yes, I can believe it. I loved your mom very much, but sadly, she could be cruel sometimes," Dad said as Chrissy walked into the kitchen and sat down on a barstool next to Dad. She wanted to hear stories that she had never heard before. "I remember once when you were around a year old. You'd just started walking and were touching things on the coffee table after being told not to. To punish you, your mom pulled out her cigarette lighter. She flicked it once, then held the flame to your tiny little fingers, burning them. You let out a scream. I'll never forget that scream for as long as I live. It pierced right through my heart and turned my stomach."

Chrissy's eyes and mouth were wide open, staring first at Dad and then at me. She was all ears. She turned back to Dad and asked, "What'd you do, Daddy?"

"I immediately cried out to Lily's mom, 'Stop it! Now!' She removed the flame." He turned to me. "I ran and scooped you up from the floor. I did my best to comfort you," Dad said, teary-eyed.

I was so thankful that I was too young to remember what had happened, but knowing my dad had been there for me made me feel better somehow. "Thanks for trying to protect me. I'm glad I don't remember that. But I do remember my mom burning my sister Eileen's fingers, and my brother Bart's fingers too. And, my mom always had such a cruel smile on her face when she was making us cry, like some part of her was actually enjoying it, you know?" Dad nodded. He knew that look too. "How does a mother do that to her own kids, Dad?" I asked. Chrissy and I stared at our dad, waiting for him to speak. We both really wanted to know the answer to that question.

"I don't know, Lily. I just don't know." Dad shrugged, looked down, and shook his head. I looked down at the floor and shook my head too. Chrissy, still shocked by the stories she had just heard, sat still and speechless.

A few minutes later Chrissy came over to me. "Lily, I'm so sorry you had such a mean mommy," she said, hugging me. I hugged her back, realizing I had made the right choice to stay over the night before. Right then I decided to stay permanently.

"Speaking of your mom," Dad said, "how is she?"

"I don't know," I replied.

"You mean you haven't spoken to her?" he asked.

"No," I replied, "not since I ran away." I pictured her getting ready that morning in her new bathroom in Idaho. I imagined an ashtray with a lit Pall Mall cigarette and a coffee cup with red lipstick smudges on the rim as she stood in front of the mirror, teasing her big bouffant hairdo. I saw her wild and long hair trailing down her back as she peered into the mirror to freshen up her lipstick one last time. I could almost smell the cigarette smoke, Aqua Net, and White Shoulders perfume.

I didn't want to call Mom, ever, but Dad said I needed to call her and let her know I was okay. "You know your Mom's worried sick about you," Dad said. I didn't care if she was, but if Dad thought it was best for me to call her, then I would. I was already starting to trust him.

I went upstairs to call my mom like Dad had asked me to. Dad and Betty's bedroom was quieter and more private than the busy kitchen downstairs. I didn't have Mom's number, but I did have my favorite uncle's number. He always seemed to know where his little sister was and how to contact her. After a short chat, he gave me her new home number in Idaho. My finger trembled slightly as I dialed.

"Hi, Mom, it's me," I said. "I'm just calling to let you know I'm fine, and living with *my* dad."

"What!?" Mom yelled so loudly I had to pull the phone receiver away from my ear. "You can't live with your father!"

Was she serious? Did she not remember I hated living with her so much that I had to run away, that I sure as hell couldn't live with her either?

I thought back to four years earlier when I had been picked up by the Santa Cruz police for running away, and brought back home. Mom motioned me to sit next to her on the wide overstuffed living room couch. She had dark circles under her red, puffy eyes, and her long, thick hair was disheveled, like she'd just tumbled out of bed. "Lily, what do you want?" she asked. "What would it take to make you happy here at home so you don't run away again?"

Me? Did I hear her right? Is she really asking me what I want? What would make me happy? I thought. This was not something I was used to being asked. I quickly answered, "I don't want to be grounded all the time, watching from my bedroom window as my friends play outside. I want to be outside playing with them. I want to be able to talk to my friends on the phone. I want to be free to go places with my friends or just hang out with them." I watched as Mom sat quietly listening and nodding, so I continued. "I don't want to be hit anymore. Oh, and I want my bedroom door back so I can have some privacy." (She had taken away my door because she said I spent way too much time in my room, and she wanted to see exactly what I was up to.)

"Okay, so that's what you want?"

"Yes, that's what I want," I said, as I heard my one-year-old baby brother (Carlos's biological son) Bart's gurgles and squeals coming from his bedroom as he played. I really wanted Carlos to leave me alone too, but I couldn't tell my mom that.

My mom got up, walked calmly to the kitchen where my seven-year-old little sister Eileen (Jeffrey's biological daughter) sat at the table eating her lunch, got a stepstool, opened the uppermost kitchen cabinet door, stepped up on the stool, reached behind the mixing bowls on the highest top shelf, and pulled out a gun.

"Okay, so you want to do whatever you want? Well, you just go right ahead, but I will not be here to watch!" Mom screamed, her wild eyes staring at me as she put the gun to her temple, threatening to pull the trigger. "And when the police come, you can explain why your mother did this. You be sure to tell them how you insisted on having your own way. You had to do whatever *you* wanted and your mother was *not*, I repeat *not* going to have any part of it. Yes, you can explain how poor Miss Lily had to have her own way as they're scrubbing my brains off the wall!"

My legs turned to jelly, and I fell to the floor sobbing. I screamed, "Mom! Please, put the gun down! Please!" I feared the inevitable gunshot blast and visualized her head exploding into little pieces, her blood and brain tissue scattered all over the kitchen. After I took back every last word I had said, swearing I'd never want anything, ever, if she would just put the gun down, she slowly lowered the gun. From then on, I didn't talk much to my mom. I was always afraid I'd say the wrong thing, and she'd pull out that gun again, only this time she would pull the trigger and kill herself—and it would be all my fault.

"Lily, did you hear what I said?" Mom asked over the phone. Her familiar harsh and raspy voice jarred me back to the present. "You can't live with your father!"

"Why not?"

"Cuz he's a *child molester!*"

"What? Mom, calling my dad a child molester is a very cruel thing for you to say!" I said, shocked. I knew my mom didn't like my dad, but I'd never heard her call him a child molester before. "You're just mad cuz I ran away and have done fine without you. I never did come crawling back to you, like you said I would. Instead, I found my dad, and I like him. I'm happy living here."

"No! I'm telling you the truth, Lily," Mom insisted. "Your father *is* a child molester! He molested you. Why do you think I divorced him?"

"I don't know, Mom. Why do you divorce anybody?" I asked sarcastically. "Maybe the problem isn't with the men you marry, maybe the problem is with you!"

"How dare you!"

"Whatever. I just called to let you know I'm fine. I have to go. Bye." I slammed the phone down.

I sat on the edge of Dad and Betty's bed and tried to calm down. After talking to my mom on the phone, I quickly remembered how glad I was to finally be away from her. I couldn't believe what my mom had said about my dad being a child molester. Could it be true? Was my dad really a child molester? No, of course not—I had no such memories.

I wondered if my mom was crazy. Soon after that gun incident when I was twelve, my mom got drunk, deliberately drove her car into the side of the mountain, and got locked up in a psychiatric ward. She was emotionally disturbed then and I began to wonder if she still was now. How could I trust anything she said? Was she even sane? She must be lying about my dad, but why? I had to ask my dad about it.

I pulled myself together and walked downstairs. My dad was alone in the kitchen. He wanted to know how my mom was doing and what she had to say. "Mom's doing fine." I paused, then took a deep breath and continued. "She says you molested me. Is that true?"

Without hesitation Dad looked me in the eye and asked, "Well, Lily, what do you think?"

"I don't think so, but I wanted to ask you. Why would my mom say that?" I said, confused.

I stared at my dad, wondering why he wasn't angry at my mom for accusing him of something like that. I would've been furious. But he just sat there looking very calm and relaxed. Then he leaned forward and said, "One evening when you were a year and a half old, I was giving you a bath. Your mom walked in and saw me washing your private area. She accused me of molesting you. I told her she was crazy, that I was just giving you a bath. But she wouldn't listen to reason, and she left me. Yeah, like I'd ever do something like that to my own daughter," Dad said, shaking his head.

I nodded. I believed my dad, and I believed he was a good parent, a caring parent, and without a doubt the better parent.

I had always thought Dad was a good parent. I remembered back to one Saturday morning when I was five. My dad had picked me up from my mom's house—they shared custody—and brought me to his. We sat on the living room floor and played Candy Land. "A sweet little game for sweet little folks like you," Dad said. It was so much fun, laughing and being silly and just hanging out with my dad.

Later that morning I jumped on my radiant sky blue Schwinn

Breeze, a special gift given to me by my dad, and headed to our neighborhood mom-and-pop grocery store. I called my bike Blue Breeze or just Breeze for short. She was a beautiful bicycle with a blue and white seat, white-walled tires, and a basket and bell. An old Queen of Hearts playing card attached to the fender brace with a clothespin slapped against the front spokes as I rode, sounding like a loud engine.

I arrived at our small grocery store, carefully balanced Breeze on the sometimes shaky kickstand, and entered the store. There was every type of food item, piled higher than I was, stretching endlessly down the maze of aisles. I casually wandered over to my favorite aisle, the candy aisle, stopped in front of the Fizzies, looked around, saw no adults, took the candy, and walked out of the store. I jumped on Breeze and headed home, so thrilled to have these delicious root beer-flavored Fizzies in my little hands.

Later that afternoon Dad found out that I had stolen the Fizzies. It was the first time I had been caught doing something wrong, and I had no idea what my dad was going to do to me. Was he going to yell at me? Hit me? Or worse yet, hate me forever for what I'd done?

"Okay, Lily," he said, without raising his voice, "let's go and return those to the store."

At the market, my dad told the store clerk what I'd done, then asked me to return the Fizzies. I slammed the packet of Fizzies down on the check-out counter, mad that I had gotten caught stealing and even madder that I really had to give them back. I wanted to keep them.

The soft-spoken clerk tried to get me to understand that it was wrong to steal. When he asked me how I'd feel if he came to my house and stole my dolls, I said, "Go right ahead! I wouldn't care!" He looked at me bewildered, not knowing how much I hated dolls. But when my dad told the clerk to ask me how I'd feel if he stole my bicycle, my Blue Breeze, the most treasured thing I owned, I cried. I couldn't even imagine how sad I'd be if someone *touched*, let alone *took*, my precious Breeze. The mere thought made me feel sick to my stomach.

Dad gave me a stern look and asked, "Lily, do you have something you'd like to say to this gentleman?"

I slowly looked over at the clerk, and with watery eyes said, "I'm sorry, Sir, for stealing your Fizzes. I'll never do it again. I promise."

On the quiet drive home, I wondered what my punishment for stealing the Fizzies was going to be. Once home my dad was very kind, as if he knew how bad I felt, and said, "Okay, Lily, I think you've learned your lesson. We don't need to discuss this anymore." He gave me a hug and then sent me outside to play.

I never forgot the two valuable lessons I learned that day. First, I understood to the very core of my being why stealing was wrong and never stole another pack of Fizzies again. Second, I didn't have to be afraid anymore of what my dad would do to me if he found out I had done something wrong. I trusted his punishments would always be fair. I believed my dad was a good parent and also the better parent because he didn't scream, beat, belittle, or punish me like my mom would have. I believed a good parent would never molest a child. So, I did not believe my mom's accusations that my dad was a child molester.

After I moved in, Dad and I quickly became best friends and got really close, really fast. He allowed me to stay out of school for the rest of the year if I promised I'd go back the next year and graduate. This allowed us to spend even more time together.

Dad proudly introduced me to everyone. At his office he introduced me to his legal secretary Jill, a tall blue-eyed blonde, and the attorneys who shared the large office with him. We walked across the street to the courthouse where he introduced me to clerks and judges and more attorneys. I wondered if somebody was going to ask me where I'd been all these years. Luckily nobody did. It felt really good to be accepted by all these people, and as I stood by my dad's side listening to him talk PI business with his clients, I felt proud to be his daughter.

One morning, a few days after I'd moved in, I was sitting next to Dad on the living room couch, drinking a cup of coffee and smoking a cigarette. Dad took a sip of coffee from his "World's Greatest Dad" mug, then asked, "So, Lily, do you have a favorite band?"

Without hesitation, I replied, "Led Zeppelin."

"Well then, let's hear some Led Zeppelin," he said as he reached over and placed his hand on my knee. I looked at him, unsure of what to think. We barely knew each other. Part of me felt uncomfortable with this sort of affection, but I didn't say anything. Maybe that was just how my dad was.

"Really? Okay, I'll go get it." I had no idea what he would think of my music, but I was eager to play my *Physical Graffiti* album. I watched him, gauging his reaction, hoping he would like it as much as I did. To my surprise, I saw my dad's foot begin tapping to the beat of the music. He said he *really* liked it, and I was floating on cloud nine when we sat and listened to the whole double album together.

Later that week Dad and I were talking, and the subject of drugs came up. "Do you have a favorite drug?" Dad asked.

"Well, yes—speed," I answered. Never in my wildest dreams could I have imagined having an open and honest conversation about drugs with an adult, let alone a parent. And yet here I was telling my dad things only my closest friends knew.

"Why?" he asked.

"Because I love the high, the way it makes me feel."

"Well, I've never tried speed, but I'd like to. The next time you've got some, can I take it with you?"

"No!"

"Why not?"

"Because, Dad, you're diabetic."

"So?"

"So, I don't think you're supposed to mix insulin and speed. It might really mess you up, or even kill you," I said, wondering why he would want to do something like that.

"If it's good enough for my daughter, it's good enough for me. So, next time you're doing speed, promise you'll share some with your dear old dad," he pressed.

"Ah … I don't know if …" I mumbled and hesitated.

"Lily, promise," he insisted.

"Okay, okay, I promise," I said. Wow, he really was serious. But all I could think about was if I gave him speed, it would probably kill him. I couldn't live with myself if that happened. Right then I decided I'd never take speed again.

The next month at my dad's, I was happy. As winter slowly turned to spring, Dad and I were together almost twenty-four hours a day, a lot of the time alone. Most days I went with him to his PI office, learning all about his work. I would drive with him when he served legal papers and sit with him during surveillances. We would grab lunches out and sometimes dinners too. At night we would stay up late watching TV together after everyone else had gone to sleep. And when I couldn't stay up a second longer, he would give me a hug and a kiss on the cheek before I headed off to bed. Sometimes he would hug me a bit too tightly, but I would never say anything. The truth was I didn't know what to say. Did I like it? Back then I was so confused, I wasn't sure what I felt. So I'd just say goodnight and try not to think about it.

The one thing I did know for sure was that my boyfriend Vance didn't make me feel special and loved the way my dad did, so I broke up with him. Slowly, I lost touch with my friends. There was no one I liked spending time with more than my dad.

Dad taught me how to drive a stick shift in his Datsun pickup. Every night for about a week and a half, he'd drive me to a vacant parking lot where we would begin the driving lessons. I'd sit behind the wheel feeling nervous, having no idea what I was doing, afraid I might damage or destroy my dad's truck. He'd slide in right next to me, place my hand on top of the smooth leather gear shift knob, and go through all the positions, showing me how to shift gears. It felt good, almost familiar somehow, having him near me, teaching me, touching me.

It seemed impossible to get that perfect balance between clutch and gas pedal—I would get so frustrated as the truck lurched forward in quick rabbit hops. "Ouch!" Dad would yell as he grabbed his neck in pain, joking that I had given him a severe case of whiplash and he might have to sue, making me bust out laughing.

Even worse was when the little yellow truck would stall. I'd yell and scream as I hit the steering wheel in anger, ready to quit. My dad would put his hand on my shoulder, or sometimes my leg, and offer me words of encouragement mixed with humor, and I couldn't help but smile and try again.

After I learned how to drive, I acquired my learner's permit and signed up for the required behind-the-wheel training at the local high school. On the second day of class, the teacher, Mr. Stanford, sat next to me as I drove. I listened intently to his every word, thrilled, knowing I would soon obtain a driver's license of my very own. Suddenly, he placed his hand on my right knee. *What the hell is he doing?* I felt like I was going to be sick. I glanced quickly in my rearview mirror, wondering if any of the other students might be aware of what was going on. All I saw were kids buckled safely in the backseat, oblivious to the teacher's inappropriate actions. *Great*, I thought. *Now what?* As I nervously maneuvered the automobile through the residential streets, he continued to maneuver his hand up my leg—all while calmly guiding me as I drove. He was teaching me defensive driving techniques when what I really needed was defensive driving instructor techniques. When he finally asked me to pull over and park the car so that the next student could take a turn behind the wheel, he announced, "Feel free to come by my office anytime, Lily."

"Yeah, thanks." *What a jerk*, I thought. I immediately ran to my dad in tears. I felt angry at the teacher for what he had done, and disappointed that now I was unable to get my driver's license because I refused to return and complete the course. My dad went with me to the principal's office. There I explained what had happened. The principal listened and then talked with Mr. Stanford who, of course, adamantly denied the allegation. With no other witnesses, it came down to my word against his. The principal proceeded to tell me that although he was sorry about my "alleged" unfortunate predicament, Mr. Stanford had worked at the school for many years. He was a fine, well-loved teacher and had never had any previous complaints against him. Therefore, as the principal, he would have to stand by his teacher. He claimed he was sorry, but there was nothing he could do.

I was *so* infuriated that the principal had done absolutely nothing to punish the instructor's despicable behavior, and outraged that the clearly guilty Mr. Stanford had gotten off scot-free for his crime. My dad comforted and reassured me. "Lily, don't worry about it. We'll take care of that asshole."

The next night Dad gave Eric and me several rolls of toilet paper and two cans of spray paint. Dad drove us past Mr. Stanford's house, parked a few doors down, killed the engine and lights, and waited while Eric and I spray painted the teacher's house and car, and toilet papered his yard. When we got home, Eric and I placed prank calls to Mr. Stanford until his phone was disconnected. A few days later we sent a used condom, donated by Eric, in a thank-you card to Mr. Stanford's residence. In the card we wrote: "Thanks for the sex, you beast you. I am returning your condom as a keepsake of our hot & sweaty night together. See you real soon. Love Always, Your Sweetie Candy. XOXO." I chuckled to myself, imagining Mr. Stanford opening the letter and reading it while his wife stood near wondering what the hell was going on as she breathed in the foul stench of stale semen. How would he explain all of this to his wife? I felt so much better knowing Mr. Stanford had paid for his unwelcome, inappropriate behavior—all courtesy of Dad, Eric, and me. At that time, I thought my dad was the greatest—my protector, my hero, my best friend. In my eyes he was perfect and could do no wrong.

Once I obtained my driver's license, I was given the responsibility of court runner for my dad's PI business. I couldn't believe that I was being trusted to pick up and drop off legal documents. *Me?* Did my dad know that I had never even held a job before? Heck, my own mom hadn't even trusted me to babysit the neighbor's children because she felt I was not responsible enough. And yet here I was—immersed in this new, mysterious world of performing stakeouts and surveillances, locating missing persons and hidden assets, dealing with judges and attorneys, and spending time in courthouses and judges' chambers.

During all this time spent with my dad, I told him my secrets and innermost thoughts, things I had never shared with anyone else before, not even my closest friends. I told him about my complicated feelings concerning my mom and how her abuse had hurt me, how sometimes I didn't care about myself, and how I often felt worthless. Dad was always there to give me much needed insight, and I always felt better after our talks.

But it was more than that. It was the way he listened so attentively to me, hanging on my every word, when no one else seemed to care much about what I had to say. It was the way his eyes could see right through me, to my very core. At first I felt exposed and vulnerable, unable to hide from him because he knew exactly what I was thinking and feeling. But that soon changed when I found that I really liked being seen and understood like that. It was like he instantly knew who I was and what I needed, and even on my bad days, my bitchy days, he didn't judge me or yell at me or beat me. He just loved me.

Dad knew exactly what he was doing. Maybe he understood me

too well. He knew how much I needed to be loved and how to take advantage of me and manipulate me.

I was beginning to have strong feelings for my dad. Although we'd been reunited for only a month and a half, it felt like my dad was not only my best friend, but also my Prince Charming, the man I'd been searching for my whole life. I felt myself falling madly in love with him, and I began to wonder if my feelings were normal. Did other teenage girls fall in love with their dads too, or was I the only one?

One night my dad encouraged me to lie on the couch with him, my head resting in his lap as we watched *The Tonight Show.* As Johnny got to know his guests better, Dad and I got to know each other better too. For an instant I wondered what his penis looked like—resting under my head. But I quickly banished that thought from my mind.

Chapter 4
MADLY IN LOVE

One morning in early April, Connor came running into my room to wake me up for the motorcycle trip to Hollister Hills State Vehicular Recreation Area. He was so excited about going and riding the new bike he'd gotten for Christmas that he couldn't stop talking about it. He'd been looking forward to it for weeks.

"Well, Lily, are you excited to go bike riding?" he asked.

"Sure, Connor," I said, wiping the sleep from my eyes. I felt more apprehensive than excited because I had no riding experience, but Dad had invited me, so I would go and give it a try.

Betty, wearing a long pink chiffon nightgown and robe, stood in the doorway and waved goodbye as Dad, Connor, Eric, and I headed off to Hollister. The sun was shining brightly when we entered the park an hour later. We followed the main road over rolling green hills freckled with bright yellow and orange wildflowers, lined on both sides with mature oak trees. Then we turned left onto a one-way dirt road and followed the signs to Walnut Camp.

The guys set up camp and were eager to ride. Connor looked more like a superhero than an eleven-year-old boy in his full protective gear: a black and red helmet and goggles, a long sleeve jersey with built-in padding and riding pants, a pair of black kneepads, elbow pads, red gloves, and heavy black boots. Eric wore a white t-shirt and jeans with his blue and silver helmet and goggles. The boys took off down the trail, their back wheels spraying dirt and loose stones behind them. Connor and Eric were daredevils, riding only difficult diamond trails. I, on the other hand, rode only the easier green dot trails. I was scared to death that I would fall or hurt myself. Dad always rode close behind me in case I got into trouble or needed encouragement. Sometimes I liked the feeling of cruising down a flat grassy area in first gear. But sometimes sitting on my bike was even better than riding it, like when I spotted a flock of wild turkeys beyond the screen of trees and Dad and I stopped to watch them feeding in a grassy patch. Now that's what I called fun.

Camping at the park was fun too. That night was quiet and peaceful with all the vehicles parked and resting, awaiting sunrise. I marveled at how comfortable and relaxed I felt. It was hard to believe that I had found my dad only two short months before. Eric lit a joint of sensimilla, took a few hits, and passed it to me. I took a deep drag and passed it to my dad, who smiled as he took it from my hand. Dad, Eric, and I passed around the joint until there was nothing left. Soon everything started to spin around me, a quick reminder of why I didn't like pot. Feeling stoned and dizzy, I cautiously made my way across the sleeping bags, which were arranged side by side, until I arrived at mine at the far left side of the tent. Connor was already fast asleep on the far right side of the tent. Dad and Eric stayed up for a while chatting.

Later that night, I lay awake, wishing I hadn't smoked that joint. The tent spun like I was riding a Tilt-A-Whirl, and I thought I was going to be sick. I wanted to sleep it off, but when I closed my eyes the tent spun even faster, making me feel worse than I already did. As I was lying there, hoping the high would wear off soon so I could finally get some sleep, I heard the zipper on my sleeping bag unzip. Then I felt something inside my bag. It took me a minute to realize my dad's hand had crept into my sleeping bag. Shocked, I froze. I felt his fingers wiggle their way into my panties and swiftly, as if by accident, graze over my clit. Then as quickly as his warm hand had entered, it retreated.

Lying awake that night, I wrestled with my mixed feelings. On the one hand, I wanted him in the *worst* way. My desire had been building up for quite a while during our time spent together. I thought about all the love, the attention, and the close physical contact between us. God I *loved* him. There I'd said it. Or should I say I finally admitted it to myself. There was no one I wanted to be with more. On the other hand, he was my dad, and I didn't want to ruin the relationship we had built. I didn't want to do anything to mess up what had been the best thing in my life.

My conflicting feelings and confusion, along with the silence in the tent, were almost unbearable. After a restless night tossing and turning, I awoke to find myself alone and in an awkward predicament. *How am I supposed to act after last night? What am I supposed to say?* I wondered. I unzipped the tent flap a few inches and peered out. My dad was standing in front of the grill flipping pancakes with a spatula in one hand and a cup of coffee in the other. I approached him hesitantly. When our eyes met, I looked away. Connor and Eric were sitting at a picnic table under a huge oak tree laughing and joking about who had had the better time around the track yesterday. "Well, good morning, sleepy head," Dad said with a cheerful voice and a smile. "Would you like some breakfast?"

"Ah ... yeah, I would, thanks." *Oh, I get it—we'll just act like last night never happened. Maybe he feels like he made a mistake, and I should forget all about it.* For the rest of the trip my dad acted as if nothing out of the ordinary had happened. The rest of the day was just like the day before. Eric and Connor couldn't wait to ride their bikes back to the main MX track and do some racing before heading home. Dad and I kept to the easy green dot trails. He still encouraged me every step of the way. And I especially needed to hear his calm, caring voice when I felt stupid, like when I confused the throttle for the brake or couldn't find the brake or forgot how to downshift. Why the guys thought this was fun escaped me. I just wanted to go home.

When we arrived home, tired and dirty, Connor and Eric began unloading the bikes while Dad and I headed inside. In the kitchen I could hear Betty yelling and cursing at Dad. I had no idea why she was so angry, the polar opposite of how she had been when we left for Hollister. As I stood in the kitchen doorway watching, Betty hurled a dinner plate at Dad. He ducked, and the plate came inches from hitting his head. "Geez, calm down," Dad said, which only seemed to piss Betty off even more.

"Fuck you!" she yelled like a crazy person as she reached for another dish to throw at him.

I looked at Dad, confused. He looked at me and said, "Lily, let's go." I nodded. We left.

My dad drove me to a secluded area on top of a nearby hill overlooking the city lights. He parked the truck, and we began to talk.

"What's wrong with Betty?" I asked.

"Lily, please don't worry about Betty. I'll deal with her, okay?"

"Okay, Dad."

"I thought we should talk about what happened in the tent," Dad said.

I paused. "Okay."

"I'm sorry I touched you. I shouldn't have done that," my dad said. I felt embarrassed and looked away, unsure of what to say. "I know about you and your stepfather, Carlos," he continued, "and I'm so sorry he did those terrible things to you." Carlos had molested me from the ages of eleven to thirteen.

My mouth dropped open in shock. "What? How...how'd you know that?" Very few people knew about it.

He just smiled and said, "Your uncle told me."

"My...uncle? Which uncle? My mom's brother?"

"Yes, Lily. After the adoption, he kept tabs on you for me. He kept me informed about how you were doing, and what you were doing." I couldn't believe my ears. I started to cry. "There, there, come on, now," he said, handing me a tissue. "You didn't think your dad would just walk away and abandon you, did you?" I slowly shook my head as I wiped the tears from my eyes. Until that moment, it was exactly what I had thought.

"Your uncle also told me you ran away from home. Why—to escape Carlos?"

I nodded, "Yeah, and Mom too, of course."

"Well, of course," Dad said. He knew all about Mom's abuse.

My dad and I had never talked about Carlos—until now. "Can you believe that when I got thrown in juvie for running away, I actually felt safer there than at home?"

"Really? Why's that?"

"Cuz there I was locked in, protected by police officers and cameras, and Carlos was locked out, unable to get in and have his way with me like he did at home. I slept far better there in my bare little cell, curled up on a cold concrete bunk, than I ever did in my own bed."

Dad looked down and shook his head in disgust. "Again, I'm so sorry for what he did to you, and I'm so sorry I wasn't there to protect you."

I felt my blood boil with anger. "Oh! I hate him! I hate that fucking asshole, Dad!" I screamed as I thought of Carlos, the man I hated most in the world, lying naked in my bed next to me, forcing me to satisfy his sexual needs. "I hated him when he touched me, when he looked at me, and even when he spoke to me. I'd always wish he'd just hurry up and die, or Mom would just hurry up and divorce him, and I'd never have to see him again. Dad, just thinking about him still makes my stomach hurt. I've never hated anyone more."

"Yes, I understand," he said in a soft but serious voice, "and I'd never want you to feel that way toward me."

"No. I'd never feel that way toward you. That situation was completely different. I didn't want to be with him, but with you—well—it's very, very different. You care about me, you love me, and you understand me. You're *nothing* like Carlos. I could never hate you—not ever."

"Okay, I just want to be clear that I'd never do anything to hurt you. Do you know that, Lily?"

"Yes, Dad, I know, I know."

"And I'd never do anything that you didn't want me to. I'm so sorry that I got carried away and touched you in the tent. I promise it will never happen again—unless you want it to. I love you, and you've already been through so much. So, you let me know what you want," Dad said, never saying what he wanted.

"I love you, Dad. I mean I *really* love you. It's okay with me if you want to touch me again like you did in the tent. I want to be with you."

"Okay, as long as you're sure," he said.

"Totally sure," I said with complete confidence.

Next, I thought he would reach over and touch me, hold me, maybe even kiss me to prove beyond a shadow of a doubt that he did indeed want me as much as I wanted him. Instead, we drove home, listening to tunes and talking about anything but, as if our entire conversation had never happened. I felt confused, unsure if I had dreamt the whole thing.

When Dad and I returned home that night, Betty was sitting on the couch in her dark green nightgown. She had an absentminded look on her face and was petting a young silver tabby cat with amber eyes. She was drinking vodka on the rocks.

My dad announced to Betty that he would be taking me the next day to his friend's cabin in Lake Tahoe for the weekend—to spend some much-needed "quality time" with his daughter. Betty nodded without looking up. She must have felt tired and drained after her outburst earlier. Her face was pale and her eyes were swollen half shut. Although I didn't want to think about it, I felt bad for her.

I also didn't want to think about how very wrong it felt to sneak behind her back. I didn't want to hurt her. But this was my dad's idea, so how wrong could it be? Besides, the mere thought of being all alone with my dad sent chills up and down my spine. To lessen my pangs of guilt, I told myself not to worry about it because, like Dad had always said, Betty was his concern, not mine. And if our trip was okay with Dad, then it was okay with me too.

Early the next morning I had my little suitcase packed and ready to go. I wore my favorite skin-tight Palmetto jeans (the same pair I had worn when I ran away from Mom) and a new powder blue t-shirt I had found when shopping with Betty. It had a cute cartoon-like cat on the front with a caption below it that read "Pet Me." I hoped Dad would get the hint.

As we drove to the cabin, we talked about everything except what we'd be doing once we got there. So many questions flooded my mind. *Is he going to touch me like he touched me in the tent the other night? But he's my dad. What does he look like naked? But he's my dad. What would it be like to really kiss him? But he's my dad. If I really do this, then what happens?* Well, I would soon find out.

The cozy A-frame cabin owned by Dad's best friend was located on a quiet mountain road, secluded on all sides by beautiful towering pine trees. Even though the sky was blue and the sun was shining, it was cold and the ground was covered in a blanket of snow from a storm that had passed through earlier that day. In the front yard stood a huge pine tree with glistening snow hung heavily on the branches, clinging like it did to the cabin's green roof. I followed Dad up the steep wooden stairs, slippery with ice and snow, to the small side door, holding onto the rail and Dad to prevent myself from falling. It was so quiet I could hear Dad's keys jingling as he searched for the right one. I could even hear my own heart beating. I couldn't tell if I was more nervous or excited to finally be alone with him.

I stepped inside and looked around. There was knotty pine throughout, with open beam ceilings, wooden shutters, and an inviting wood burning fireplace. It was cold in the cabin, so Dad lit a fire in the fireplace and motioned me to come and stand next to him. He wrapped his arms around me and held me as close as he could to warm me up. "Better?" he asked.

"Better," I said, the goosebumps that had been covering my arms from the cold chill in the air now gone. He took my face in his hands and said softly, "I love you, Lily." Then he kissed me. Not a peck-on-the-cheek sort of kiss either, but an intense and passionate kiss with his lips pressed hard against mine. I had never been kissed like that before. The kiss took my breath away. I finally knew he hungered for me too.

He took my hand and led me down the hallway to the master bedroom where he laid me gently on the bed and undressed me. As he lay next to me touching and exploring my body, I wondered why he still had all his clothes on. I wanted to touch him too, but I didn't want to ruin this perfect moment by saying anything. I felt tiny goosebumps racing across my skin, chasing after his fingertips as they brushed over me, erupting not from the cold chill in the air as before but from the heat of his touch. My dad knew just the right way to tease me, touch me, and pleasure me like I had never been before. I thought he must be a real gentleman because he had put my sexual needs before his own.

I couldn't help but stare when Dad finally undressed. He caught me staring, smiled, and said I could touch him if I wanted to, so I did. I'd had my fair share of boyfriends, but they were inexperienced—I had found most were more concerned with their own orgasms than mine and didn't have much interest or skill needed to pleasure me. My dad, on the other hand, gave me sexual experiences far beyond my wildest dreams.

Needless to say, we couldn't keep our hands off each other,

engaging in long love-making sessions throughout our weekend together. I did take occasional breaks to catch my breath—the thin air of high-altitude Tahoe got to me sometimes—but then I was eager to continue our love fest. I found his body luscious, and his sexual talents titillating, taking my breath away each and every time.

During our stay at the cabin, Dad and I could talk freely without worrying about someone overhearing us. He told me how miserable he had been. Connor and Chrissy looked at him as a walking dollar sign, which saddened him. With tears in his eyes, he told me that he was unhappy in his marriage and didn't love Betty anymore. He said he didn't enjoy having sex with her anymore. Actually, he hadn't really enjoyed anything anymore until I came back into his life. He'd felt dead inside, but now he felt alive and happy, and it was all because of me. *Me.* He loved me. I was his "sweet lovey-dove," and he loved me like he had never loved anyone else before, more than life itself. And he would do anything for me because he never wanted to lose me, ever.

As he lit a cigarette, I stared at him. He didn't look like I imagined a thirty-nine-year-old man would. He didn't look, well, old. I didn't see any wrinkles on his skin, and his body was tan and firm and fit, with an energy level equal to mine.

I didn't see him as my father—my boyfriend and older lover, yes, but my father, heavens no. I hadn't grown up with him and barely even remembered him from my childhood. He was not like my stepfather Carlos whom I had seen as a father, whom I had grown up with, and who had forced me to sleep with him as a child. For Carlos I felt only hate. But for my dad I felt only love.

Dad told me our being together couldn't be wrong if we both loved each other the way we did. I agreed. "We can't choose who we fall in love with, now can we, Lily?" Dad asked, his big chocolate brown eyes looking into mine. All I'd ever wanted was to be loved like everyone else. Lying next to him, skin to skin, I believed I finally was. How could that possibly be wrong?

On the drive home Dad told me the plan. For now we would act like nothing had happened. We would act as we had before our trip to Tahoe, like any other dad and daughter did. But very soon we'd be together and wouldn't have to sneak around anymore. Because the plan was Dad would ask Betty for a divorce. Then, I would live with my dad, while Connor and Chrissy would live with Betty. This arrangement would allow Dad and me to spend lots more time together, alone. I loved the idea, and Dad couldn't wait either. All my confusion vanished once my dad had finally defined our relationship. I felt relieved and safe knowing he would take care of everything now. Like most teens, I never thought much about the future.

The next night, after our return from Tahoe, I sat at the kitchen table with Connor on one side of me and Chrissy on the other. Across the table sat Dad, Betty, and Eric. As I passed the spaghetti to Connor, I looked up at my dad. It was so hard to pretend that I wasn't madly in love with him, that I didn't want to jump right over the stupid table and kiss him. I imagined his tongue teasing mine.

"Lily, do you want some garlic bread?" Connor asked, shattering my perfect moment. I knew Dad and I would be alone soon, and the waiting would only make our secret, sexual escapades that much more intense, if that were possible.

It was not easy to return home and pretend that nothing had happened. But there were Betty, Connor, Chrissy, Eric, and the whole world who knew us as "father and daughter," so as hard as it was sometimes, we acted our appropriate parts when we had to. I thought once Dad divorced Betty, and Dad and I were finally free to be together, life would be perfect.

Chapter 5
BETTY

Shortly after our trip to Tahoe, Dad told me that he had asked Betty for a divorce, and promised me that we'd be together very soon. The following night I sat next to my dad on the couch watching our favorite TV show, *The Tonight Show*, when Betty came stomping down the stairs with a bottle of vodka in her hand. She stood there glaring at Dad. "Well? Where the hell have you been, asshole? I've been waiting all this fucking time for you to come upstairs and go to bed. Well then, fuck you!" She hurled the bottle against the kitchen wall, shattering it. I watched the alcohol drip down the wall and form patterns that looked like abstract art. As quickly as Betty had entered the room, she stormed back upstairs with her fit of anger following behind her. Upstairs Connor and Chrissy slept through the ruckus.

I looked at my dad. "Lily, stay right here. I'll be right back," he said, and went upstairs. Several minutes later he returned, and we continued watching TV as if nothing had ever happened. We had made an agreement that he would handle Betty, and I was not supposed to ask questions or worry about her, so I didn't. I told myself that Dad knew best. Besides, I was just a kid—what did I know about troubled adults?

A few nights later while Dad was attending a Knights of Columbus meeting, Betty brought out the wine—sweet Mirassou Chenin Blanc. By the time Connor and Chrissy were tucked into bed, Betty and I had opened our third bottle. We were relaxing on the comfy living room couch when the phone rang.

Betty, more than a little tipsy, got up slowly, giggled, and stumbled into the shadowed kitchen to answer the phone. She covered the receiver and mouthed, "It's my friend Ruth," as she switched on the kitchen light. I nodded. Ruth lived a few doors down from us and seemed like a very nice lady. I grabbed a magazine off the coffee table and slowly flipped through the pages, not reading a word, wanting to look like I was engrossed in a story while I eavesdropped on their conversation. "Ruth, Bill's been acting very weird lately...Well, he says he's not happy anymore, says he doesn't want to be married anymore...A midlife crisis? Do you really think so?...Then, I wish he'd just go out and buy a flashy red sports car. I thought men did that, you know, to feel better..." I didn't know what a midlife crisis was, but I wanted to tell her that a car wasn't going to get Dad to stay or make him feel any better. Another minute passed. I wondered what Ruth was saying. I looked up. Betty raised one finger and mouthed, "One minute."

"Okay," I mouthed back.

Then she turned her back to me, and I heard her whisper into the phone, "You know, maybe if I had the body of a boy, Bill would love me..." I wondered what Betty meant. My mind was racing, trying to figure it out, but it didn't make any sense to me at all. Maybe this was why I shouldn't be eavesdropping in the first place. I'm sure if I could hear the whole conversation it would make perfect sense. "I have to go, Lily's here," she said and hung up the phone. She sat back on the couch, and as the wine kept flowing, so did our conversation.

"Did you know your dad wants a divorce?" Betty asked as she opened our fourth bottle of Mirassou and filled our glasses.

"Hmm...yeah, I think he mentioned something about that." Even drunk I didn't have the heart to tell her that her husband—my dad—and I were madly in love and having incredible sex, and that was a big reason why he wanted a divorce.

"I'd rather be dead."

I stared at her. "Wait—what? What did you say?"

"I said I'd rather be dead. I'd rather drive my car off a bridge and die than live without your father. I can't divorce him. I love him. Life without him is not worth living." She began to cry. "Do you understand what I'm saying?"

"Yeah, I understand."

"No, really, do you really understand, Lily? Do you?"

"Yes, Betty, I really do. You wouldn't be able to live without my dad. You love him more than anything. That's why you can't divorce him." I really did understand; I loved him too.

"That's right. I'm happy *you* understand. Now if I could just get your father to understand, too." She reached for some tissues to dry her eyes, then reached for her glass of Mirassou and took a big gulp.

After finishing my glass of wine, I said goodnight and headed upstairs to bed, all the while thinking about what Betty had said. Maybe it was the desperation in her voice, maybe it was just my gut instinct, but I believed Betty. I didn't want Betty to kill herself so that Dad and I could live together. But I couldn't imagine living without him either.

Later that night my dad came home and entered my bedroom like he always did. I was crying. He sat on the edge of my bed and took my hand. "Lily, what's wrong?"

"You can't divorce Betty. She told me she'd rather drive her car off a bridge and die than have you leave her. She can't live without you, Dad."

"Oh, come on. She isn't serious. She's just drunk. The two of you have had *way* too much to drink." He chuckled and handed me a tissue.

"No, Dad, you don't understand," I tried to explain. "She wasn't joking. She was very serious—she will kill herself if you divorce her, so you can't. Okay?"

"Lily, listen to me. I don't want you to worry about Betty, okay? Like I've said many times before, she's my wife. I'll deal with her."

"Ah, well, I don't know if—"

"Lily," Dad said, his voice stern. "Okay."

"Okay," I agreed. Suddenly, Betty came stumbling into my room, her eyes bloodshot and swollen with smudges of eyeliner and mascara beneath them. She had a large butcher knife in her hand and was waving it back and forth in the air. "I hate you! I hate you! You want a divorce? Well, asshole, I'll kill you first!"

"Betty, come on now. Calm down, you're drunk." Dad stood up and slowly approached her. "Give me the knife before you hurt yourself, okay?" He reached for the knife.

"No!" She lunged at him, aiming for his throat. I screamed. It was like something right out of a horror movie. I was terrified that Betty was going to brutally stab my dad to death while I just sat there paralyzed and watched. Dad dodged to his left, the knife missing him by a few inches. She tried again, missed, lost her balance, and staggered. Dad grabbed her wrist in a viselike grip and pried the knife out of her hand. Then he took a wailing and weeping Betty into their bedroom, closing the door behind them. I heard a lot of yelling, but after that night things seemed to calm down.

A week later, I walked into the kitchen and saw Connor looking through the fridge. He stopped and glared at me. "It's all your fault, Lily!"

"What's all my fault?"

"The divorce!" He slammed the refrigerator door. "My mom said if you hadn't moved in here, my dad wouldn't be asking her for a divorce!"

I hesitated, then took a deep breath. "What do I have to do with their divorce?"

"My mom said Dad's spending all his time with you and forgetting about us!" I shook my head and walked away, feeling relieved. Connor didn't seem to know anything about my affair with Dad, but I was scared that Betty did.

Later that day I told Dad what Connor had said. Dad told me Betty was very jealous of all the time he was spending with me, but to remember that even if I wasn't living there or having an affair with him, he'd still be getting a divorce. He didn't love Betty anymore. Hugging me, he said not to worry, Betty didn't suspect a thing, and he had already started looking around for an apartment for us to live in.

Three weeks later, almost a month and a half after Dad had asked Betty for a divorce, Eric and I sat in Dad's parked truck outside San Jose Hospital waiting to hear how Betty was doing. An hour before, Dad had gotten a call from Betty's boss at Newberry's saying that she had collapsed in the middle of her shift and had been taken to the hospital.

I lowered the passenger's side window and stared at the word EMERGENCY in big red letters above the hospital's double-glass doors, the same doors Betty had been rushed through earlier that afternoon. I wondered what had happened. Betty must have found out about the affair and tried to kill herself. It was the only explanation I could think of and the only one that made any sense to me. I imagined her collapsing on the floor at Newberry's after slitting her wrists, writhing in pain, blood everywhere.

In my mind I could still hear Connor yelling, "It's all your fault, Lily!" I believed it was all my fault. If I hadn't moved in, then Dad and I wouldn't be together, and Betty wouldn't be here struggling for her life. I wondered if I should leave, just walk away and never look back. I hated the idea of being alone, but the guilt was eating me alive. It felt far worse than any fear I had of being alone. What had I done? I grabbed the door handle, ready to flee.

"It's not your fault, you know," Eric said as he lit two cigarettes and handed me one.

"What?" I asked, shocked he could read my mind. I slowly released my grip on the door handle and took the cigarette.

"It's not you. Betty did the same thing when I first started spending time with your dad too."

I stared wide-eyed at Eric. "Huh?"

"Betty got jealous of me too, Lily. She got all worked up about it, passed out, and was taken here to the hospital. She'd hyperventilated. That's all. I bet the same thing happened today, and she'll be fine just like she was before."

"Really?"

"Yep, really. Your dad said she was doing stuff like that long before I came along, and probably would always do stuff like that. That's just how Betty is." Eric shrugged. "She's manic-depressive, you know."

"No, I didn't know...and, that's, just, well, crazy," I said, staring into his calm ocean blue eyes while inhaling deeply on my cigarette.

"You want to hear crazy?" he asked as he leaned forward and flicked his ashes into an already overfilled ashtray. "Can you believe she thought that if she had the body of a boy like me, your dad would spend more time with her?"

"No...really?" I asked.

Suddenly what I had overheard Betty say to Ruth on the phone that night about wanting the body of a boy made sense. She was jealous of Eric and had been trying to look like him. For the first time since I'd moved in, I wondered if Betty really was crazy.

"Yep. She went on a crash diet and lost lots of weight, but your dad still didn't spend more time with her. Duh," he said, and then blew a chain of smoke rings into the still air. "Like your dad always says, 'Betty's just a jealous and crazy wife. Always has been. Always will be.'"

I closed my eyes to let his words sink in. What if I had nothing to feel bad or guilty about, if all Betty's problems had nothing to do with me, or with Dad, or even with our secret affair? I felt my guilt and shame lessen, and a sense of relief washed over me. Suddenly, I sat up a little straighter, my breathing became a little easier, and my chest felt a little less tight.

Eric turned the radio on and "Hotel California" flooded the small cab. He turned the volume way up and we sang along, knowing the words by heart, not caring that we were in a hospital parking lot and shouldn't be blasting rock and roll music with our windows down. It felt good to escape in the music, get lost in the words, and forget who we were and why we were sitting there. We believed we were the lucky ones, the better ones because we would never do crazy things like Betty and wind up in the hospital. Eric and I were smarter than that, never thinking that maybe we might be victims too.

Dad came out to let us know that Betty was doing fine. She had hyperventilated and would be released from the hospital later that day. Eric had been right all along. Betty was fine just like she had been before. I believed, like Eric did, that Betty would always be fine.

At around nine o'clock the following Monday morning, my dad and I walked into the kitchen with a box of donuts we'd picked up from Christy's. Dad brewed a fresh pot of Kona coffee, poured himself a cup, and started eating some custard-filled donut holes while I was still trying to decide whether to have a chocolate bar with crème or a cinnamon roll with raisins. He asked if I could go upstairs and see if Betty would like some coffee. The request seemed somewhat unusual since I had never been asked to do that before, but it seemed simple enough. "Sure," I said.

When I got to Dad and Betty's bedroom, I opened the door and saw Betty lying in bed. She seemed semi-awake and a bit odd. Maybe she had had too much to drink the night before or hadn't slept, or maybe she wasn't feeling well, or ... *Whatever*, I thought, reminding myself she was not my problem to deal with, but Dad's. Besides, I only wanted to do what my dad had asked me to do, so I asked her if she wanted some coffee. She quietly mumbled something unintelligible, so I went over to the side of her bed and asked again. "Betty, do you want some coffee?" I could tell she was trying very hard to tell me something, but her slurred words were impossible to understand. I leaned in closer in an attempt to decipher her answer to my simple question. I asked again, speaking extra slowly and clearly. "Betty, do you want coffee—yes, or no?" She mumbled again, but no matter how hard I tried, I just couldn't make out what she was saying, so I gave up. As I began to move away from her bed, she lunged forward in an attempt to grab me, still babbling incoherently, but now her voice had a greater sense of urgency. She lunged again and inadvertently hit her nightstand, tipping it over. *Okay, this is creepy*, I thought. I knew something was wrong, but was not sure what, so without a moment's hesitation, I bolted down the stairs. "Hurry, Dad! Hurry! You need to go check on Betty! Something's wrong with her!" I yelled, trying to catch my breath.

My dad took a long sip of coffee and then asked, "What?"

"I don't know, but she can't talk and she knocked over her nightstand and...and...Dad, I think there's something really wrong with her."

"Well, does she want some coffee?" he asked as he popped a donut hole in his mouth.

"I don't know! I couldn't understand what she was saying!"

"Come on now, Lily, calm down," Dad said, smiling. "Don't worry, I'll check on her, okay?"

I took a deep breath and tried to calm down, reminding myself that my dad would deal with Betty, trusting that he knew best. "Okay, Dad," I said. Grabbing a chocolate bar with crème and a cup of coffee, I went and sat in the living room with Connor and Chrissy, who were listening to records and horsing around. After a while, I forgot all about Betty, assuming Dad had taken care of her.

About an hour and a half later Dad called me upstairs. He was walking Betty around, trying to keep her from going to sleep. "Betty swallowed a bottle of pills," he said, pointing over to the empty bottle of Valium on the bed. "I just called 911. The ambulance is on its way." My heart sank, and I wondered why my dad had waited an hour and a half before calling 911, but I didn't say anything. Part of me just didn't want to know.

Betty struggled to speak, slurring her words like she had when I'd asked her if she wanted coffee earlier that morning. I still couldn't make out what she was saying. Her eyelids were very heavy, almost closed. Dad kept talking to her, saying things like, "You shouldn't have taken all those pills, Betty," and "No, Betty, no, you can't go to sleep right now," and asking persistent repetitive questions like, "Hey, Betty, how you doing?" and "Where are you, Betty?" and "What day is it, Betty?" His voice was the only thing keeping her from going to sleep, possibly for the last time. Her body was mostly limp and barely functioning on its own, and she would have surely fallen to the ground if Dad had let her go.

I stood paralyzed, watching my dad walk a half-unconscious Betty around their bedroom, when suddenly it was my stepfather Carlos walking my half-unconscious Mom around their bedroom after her first suicide attempt five years before. Carlos was talking to my mom, asking her questions similar to those my dad was asking Betty, doing whatever it took to try to keep her awake and alive. *You can't die! Please don't die, Mom!* I'd shouted inside my head. *Please don't leave me here all alone in this house with Carlos!* I'd cried, shaking and unable to move.

The sound of sirens jolted me back to the present. Dad walked Betty downstairs, and I followed. Dad jumped into the back of the red and white ambulance with Betty, and I was to follow in Dad's truck while Connor and Chrissy stayed with Ruth. Before I pulled out of the driveway, Ruth came up to the truck. I rolled down my window and she said, "Lily, I just want you to know that none of this is your fault, okay? Betty was having serious problems long before you came along." I nodded and threw the truck in reverse to catch up with the ambulance, which was already at the end of the street. Ruth ran over to Connor and Chrissy, who stood on the front porch clinging desperately to each other. Ruth hugged them close, standing between them and the curious neighbors who had heard the sirens and had gathered, gawking, eager to hear the news of what had happened. I heard Connor yell, "But I want to go with my mom too!" and then saw him bury his face in Ruth's dress and cry, which made Chrissy cry too.

I sped up to keep up with the ambulance, repeating over and over again, "Please, dear sweet angels above, please don't let Betty die. Please save Betty's life like you did my mom's. Please."

Betty was taken to San Jose Hospital. Dad and I sat and waited. I had always hated hospitals. Everything about them gave me the creeps. They were full of pain and sadness. The smell of sickness and death seemed to linger in every corner, always hiding just beneath that sterile odor of antiseptic. Sitting there with that uncomfortable creepy feeling reminded me of when I'd gone to see my mom while she was locked up in a mental hospital when I was twelve. During my visits there, I'd been so scared that her eyes would turn dark and empty like those of the patients shuffling by us, so frightened that she would become a zombie just like them.

Before long Dad and Betty's priest, Father O'Grady, arrived and sat with us in the waiting room. Father O'Grady was a tall, slender gentleman with a kind smile, dressed in a pair of black slacks and a black shirt with a white collar. We sat in silence, waiting.

After a while a doctor came in and asked to speak with Dad alone. Moments later the same doctor appeared and motioned Father O'Grady over. I watched as they faded down the corridor.

While I sat there in the waiting room, it suddenly all made sense to me. *Oh my God! Betty's dead!* That had to be it. I thought for sure the doctor had broken the sad news to both men, and now they were strategizing the best way to gently break the news to me. The hospital walls started closing in on me like a boa constrictor, slowly squeezing the breath out of me. I gasped for air. Something inside of me knew I had to get out before I died there too, so I flew out of my chair and made a beeline for the door.

Once outside the hospital, I switched to autopilot. My legs ran as though they had a mind of their own, carrying me far away from that dreadful hospital. I needed to find somewhere, anywhere, to be alone—it felt like my whole life depended on it. At each corner I turned I found another endless row of houses that looked exactly like the last, except that their colors had changed. After frantically searching for a safe place to disappear, I finally found a parking lot that was nearly deserted. There were a few scattered cars parked up against a fence, but no people in sight. I saw a bar in the distance and could hear the faint sounds of people talking and laughing, music playing, and glassware clinking.

I curled up in a fetal position, wedging myself between an old green Oldsmobile and a fence. Completely hidden, I finally felt free to let it all out and have a much-needed mini nervous breakdown. I couldn't stop crying.

I knew Betty was dead and it was all my fault. She had told me she would rather die than live without my dad, and I had done nothing to help her. Overcome with guilt, I felt her reaching out for me, clawing at me like she had in her bed that morning. Her slurred, incomprehensible words haunted me.

I have no idea how long I was curled up there, but at some point, I dried my tears, pulled myself together as best I could, and wandered back toward the hospital. I encountered Father O'Grady near the hospital entrance. "Where have you been, Lily?" he asked, concerned.

"I needed to be alone," I said. Ashamed for all I had done and afraid a man of God would know the sins I had committed if he were to look long enough into my eyes, I kept my head down, staring at his well-worn black shoes.

"Your father and I were worried sick about you," he said, squinting into the sun. "When you left, your father thought you might have run away, and he was afraid he would never see you again."

"I'm sorry," I said.

"I told your father to stay put in case there was word about Betty," he said, "and that I would go and look for you."

"You mean," I asked, looking up at him, "Betty, isn't dead?" I had been so sure that she was.

"No, Lily," Father O'Grady said, shaking his head and shading his eyes with his hand. "Betty's not dead." He put his arm around my shoulders and led me into the waiting room where my dad sat. "I think there's someone here who really needs to see, with his own two eyes, that you're truly okay." Dad's eyes were red and watery. He smiled at me as I slid into the seat next to him.

Betty had her stomach pumped and was placed in intensive care. The doctor said most of the diazepam had already been absorbed into her system, so the prognosis wasn't good, but he also said we should never give up hope. A few hours later she fell into a coma.

Later that night we drove home. Before retiring to my bedroom, I went to say goodnight to Dad. Vivid details of that morning came rushing back as I approached Betty and Dad's bedroom. I stopped at the doorway and peered in. Dad was sitting on the side of the bed, wearing his favorite black silk robe, smoking a cigarette. He motioned me in. I fell into his open arms and cried. "It'll be okay, I promise," my dad reassured me, holding me tight, rocking me and stroking my hair. "You're tired. It's been a long day. I think you should come to bed with me and try to get some sleep," he said, patting the bed.

"Dad, no! I can't sleep in this bed. It's Betty's bed, and yours. She wouldn't want me sleeping in her bed," I said, feeling like I was going to die if I slept in that bed. "What if she dies, Dad? What if Bet—"

"Lily," he interrupted. "I know none of this has been easy for you. I know you are feeling very scared and alone right now. You probably feel like you're drowning, and no one can save you, not even me."

I sat there speechless. How did my dad always know exactly how I felt, sometimes even before I did? No one had ever known me so well. He took my face between his hands and looked into my eyes. "Lily, I love you more than I've ever loved anyone else in my entire life. I'll always be here for you. Always. I will never desert you. I will never let you down. I promise." I sniffled and smiled. His words soothed me, and I fell fast asleep in his arms.

I woke up out of a deep sleep when I heard the phone ring late that night. Terrified of the bad news I would hear if I answered it, I lay there trembling while Dad answered the phone. It was official. Betty hadn't made it through the night—she was gone. I looked at my dad. I was surprised he wasn't crying and falling apart like I was. She had been his wife for nearly fourteen years.

"Are you okay, Dad?" I asked, wiping my tears.

"No, Lily, I'm not. I'm very angry at Betty."

"Why?"

"Because she took the easy way out," Dad said, shaking his head in disgust. "She was weak and a poor excuse for a mother. No good mother would ever leave her children behind like that."

The next night Dad told me I should sleep in his room again, so after Connor and Chrissy went to sleep, I did. Early the next morning I returned to my old room so that Connor and Chrissy wouldn't know I'd slept with Dad. My old room was now my "pretend room". (Eventually I stopped sleeping in my pretend room altogether. It became a place to store my stuff and an excellent front to keep any suspicions at bay when company came over.)

Betty's funeral was the following Monday. I had never been to a funeral before and didn't want to go to Betty's, but Dad said I had to. "But, Dad, you don't understand. I'm really, really scared," I said.

"Don't be afraid," Dad said. "I'll be right there with you." I thought that was supposed to be comforting, but it wasn't. Once in the viewing room, I refused to go up and view Betty's open casket. What kind of sick and morbid tradition was that? I turned toward the rear door of the funeral home, ready to run. But Dad thought it would be a good idea for me to go up and say goodbye to Betty. He said it would make the loss more real, leaving no doubt in my mind that Betty was really gone. So with Dad's support under one arm and his sister's under the other, I was lifted up and dragged to the casket to view Betty's dead body. Because I had never seen a dead person before, I was scared and tried to keep my eyes shut. But curiosity got the best of me and I took a quick peek. I wished I hadn't looked. No matter how hard I tried, I couldn't get the image of her lying there in her coffin out of my mind.

Everyone came back to our house after the funeral. The living room was full of people, most of them family I didn't even know trying to console me. But I didn't want to talk to strangers; I wanted to be alone. I pushed past them and ran upstairs. I wasn't sure which room to go to, my pretend room or Dad's room, but I picked Dad's room, which was now our room. If someone happened to wander upstairs, find me, and wonder why I wasn't in my own room, I didn't care. The truth was, I didn't know why either. There I broke down. I still couldn't believe it. Betty was really dead. Had she known I was sleeping with her husband? Was that the reason she had killed herself? Was she happier now? Sitting on her bed staring at her favorite romance novel resting on the nightstand, I couldn't stop crying. I couldn't get rid of the guilt. It was eating me alive.

That night the nightmares began. I saw Betty's dead body lying in the coffin like it had been in the funeral home. All of a sudden her eyes opened wide. I screamed. She sat up and reached out for me, clawing at me just like she had in her bed on her last morning alive. I felt the cold touch of her scaly decaying skin brush against me. It made my skin crawl. Watching in horror as her flesh fell off her body, I struggled to get away. I was running, but I wasn't going anywhere. There was a smell of death, like rotten fish but worse. I wanted to vomit but couldn't. Betty continued to speak to me like she had the last time I'd seen her alive. I kept hearing her same desperate, incomprehensible words over and over again in my head. Then I woke up, shaking and sweaty. *Am I going stark raving mad?* I wondered. This continued every night for a long time.

Connor was devastated after his mom committed suicide. Dad said Connor was upsetting Chrissy, who was too young to fully comprehend the concept of death. Sometimes Chrissy thought her mom would be home soon and she would see her again. But when Chrissy saw Connor sad and crying, she would cry too without understanding why. Also, Connor was very angry with me, blaming me for his mom's death, wishing I had never moved in. So the day after the funeral, Dad had sent Connor to stay with Betty's family in Southern California for a few months.

There was an eerie feeling like something wasn't right about the Minx house now that Betty was gone. I looked around and everything appeared to be the same. The kitchen still opened into the dining room, separated by the breakfast bar, and the same swivel barstools sat silently tucked under the tiled countertop—the place where countless meals had been eaten, where Connor and Chrissy had their morning breakfast before school or did homework, where guests gathered or chatted. The same sunburst clock that Betty had loved hung on the dining room wall, still keeping time. The red brick fireplace and mantel were still adorned with family photos, capturing precious family memories of which I had not been a part. But without Betty, it wasn't the same.

I had a feeling that Betty's soul could not rest in peace until I was out of her house and gone from the master bedroom, where I now slept and had sex with her husband in her king-size bed. Sometimes, I could hear her voice calling out to me from her bedroom, repeating over and over again the same incoherent mumbling I'd heard the last morning I saw her alive.

If I was downstairs when I heard her, I would immediately stop everything I was doing and freeze. I would listen very hard, trying to make sense of the last slurred sounds she had uttered to me. I wanted to know what it was that she'd been trying to tell me. Had she wanted to be saved? Did she regret taking all those pills? Many times, palms sweaty and heart racing, I thought about running like hell out the front door. Sometimes I ran outside and sat on the front lawn, nervously chain-smoking until Dad got home. I felt braver walking back into the house with Dad beside me, as if he were protecting me from Betty, and from myself.

If I was upstairs when I heard her, I would run down the stairs as fast as I could, too terrified to stop and look behind me. Then I would try to calm down, sometimes needing to leave the house before I could relax.

Betty haunted me day and night. Awake or asleep, I couldn't get her voice out of my head. I felt like a crazy sixteen-year-old girl who heard the voice of a dead forty-five-year-old woman. I clung tightly to my dad. He was all I had.

"Lily. Lily, wake up. It's okay. It's just a dream. I'm here. You're safe," Dad said loudly one night. I woke up, drenched in sweat and tangled in our sheets after one of my nightmares. Dad held me until I stopped shaking. He gently stroked my hair and kissed my head. He rolled over on his left side and turned on the lamp on the nightstand.

We sat up in bed. He fluffed up two pillows, propped them against the headboard behind my back, and offered me a cigarette. Then we stayed up and talked through the night like we had most nights since Betty's funeral. I started with the nightmare. It was the same as it always had been. There were coffins. There were corpses.

And there was Betty. There was always Betty.

"I can't sleep with you anymore, Dad!" I cried out. "I just can't. It feels wrong."

"Why?" he asked calmly.

"Because, Betty's dead, and you were her husband, and, and, I'm here in her bed with you," I said. "It feels bad. It feels wrong, Dad."

"Lily," he said, staring at me, "we've had this discussion before."

"Yeah, I know we have," I said, holding back the tears, "but it's different now."

"Do you love me?"

"Yes, but—"

"No buts. Do you love me?"

"Yes," I said, looking down and tapping the ashes of my cigarette, staring as they fell helplessly into the ashtray.

"Then, there's no reason for you to feel bad, okay?" I gave him a slight nod, trying to believe it, needing to believe it so that I wouldn't feel sick to my stomach every time I lay in Betty's bed.

He continued. "We love each other, right?" I gave him a slight nod again. "No one will ever love you more than your dad, Lily. Listen to your father. You've done *nothing* wrong."

"But Betty's dead. Sometimes I feel like it's all my fault. She said she'd rather kill herself than live without you. If I hadn't been here, you would've stayed with her. She'd still be alive."

"No, I still would have left. I was not happy."

"Well, she would have lived longer then."

"Lily, do you know that Betty's death had nothing to do with you?" Dad asked.

"No. In fact, it feels like it had everything to do with me," I cried.

"I think you should know something. Betty tried to commit suicide when she was married before. Do you think that was your fault too?"

"No."

"Did you hold her mouth wide open and pour the pills down her throat?" he asked, grinning.

"No."

"Did you hold a gun to her head and tell her to start swallowing those pills right now, or else you'd shoot her dead?"

I let out a little chuckle. "No."

"You see, it wasn't your fault. It wasn't my fault. All fault lies with Betty. Got it?"

"Got it." I really didn't get it. How did he do that? How did he get me to change my mind when I'd thought my mind was already made up? Or get me to laugh again when before all I could do was cry? I didn't know how he got me to like myself again when I had hated myself and everything I had done. I lay back down, feeling much better, and fell fast asleep.

The nightmares continued every night for weeks. Some nights I didn't want to go to sleep. I tried to stay up as long as I could. I was barely staying afloat, drowning in a lake of guilt and terror. But Dad always saved me.

I know it sounds crazy, but I thought what my dad and I had was true love. I thought it was the kind of perfect love people yearn and search for their whole lives. What else could it be? What else could feel that good?

But perhaps love had nothing to do with it at all. Perhaps words like "manipulation" and "grooming" are far better words to describe it. But I didn't know those words, not yet. Back then I felt like the luckiest girl in the world to have a dad like mine to snuggle up to at night. He was my rock, my safe haven. I needed him. I loved him more than life itself.

Chapter 6
GAMES AND MANIPULATIONS

It had been just over a month since Betty had committed suicide, and I was still struggling. Dad knew he needed to get me out of the house, which I believed was haunted, and get me smiling and laughing again. And he had a pretty good idea how to do it. On July 23, 1977, Dad and I drove to the Oakland Coliseum where he surprised me with tickets to *Day On The Green #6*—with none other than *the* Led Zeppelin headlining. I was in heaven. Dad told me the tickets weren't easy to come by. "Lily, they sold out in five hours!" Dad smiled, and for the first time in a long time, I smiled too. This was my first concert ever, since my mom had forbidden me to attend such events. I had to chuckle at the irony: Here I was about to celebrate with my forbidden father and favorite rock band, and on my mom's birthday, no less.

I sat down on the grass close to the front of the stage next to Dad with a beer in one hand and a cigarette in the other waiting, just like the 54,000 other people packed in the overflowing stadium, for my idol Robert Plant to come out on stage. I was so excited to be there. Dad and I held hands. I squeezed his hand. He smiled, gave me a little wink, and squeezed my hand right back. Soon there was a restless crowd yelling, cheering, and stomping for Zeppelin. Dad and I joined in and didn't stop until the band came out. I stared at handsome Robert Plant standing confidently in the middle of the stage in his tight blue jeans and t-shirt with the caption, "Nurses Do It Better!" *Nurses, why nurses? Maybe, I do it better,* I thought, smiling. I was engulfed by Robert's powerful voice; his screams and sweet moans seemed to come from the very depths of his soul. As he continued to sing, I began to feel his voice ease my pain, soothing me like it always did. I was living in the moment, forgetting all the bad stuff and just having a blast. "Pass me another beer, Dad," I said. I loved him so much and felt even closer to him. It was a perfect day.

It was a perfect night too. For the first time since Betty's funeral, I slept through the night without haunting nightmares of Betty clawing at me, chasing me, and mumbling to me the same slurred words she had the last morning I saw her alive.

The next day Dad and I went out on a job. Dad's latest client was a father who had kidnapped his eighteen-month-old daughter Maria from his allegedly abusive and soon-to-be ex-wife earlier that morning. We flew them to Sacramento in a little blue and white Piper Cherokee plane owned by a pilot friend of Dad's. Once in Sacramento, Maria and her father had a jump on the authorities, who were busy looking for them in San Jose and the surrounding Bay Area. As I waved goodbye, sweet little Maria with the big brown eyes and wavy dark hair smiled at me. It seemed like she was thanking me for bringing her and her father together. I was happy to help make that happen because I believed she belonged with her father. I thought her father loved her like my dad loved me, and if Maria was with her father she would grow up happy and loved and safe, and could not possibly be in any sort of danger. As a naïve sixteen-year-old I thought I knew everything. I didn't. I was so clueless. What did I know? I never once thought about what her life might be like on the run, moving from place to place, with no stable home life, or how she might feel being separated from her mother and from the rest of her family. Or that maybe her father was actually the abusive parent, and now she was trapped with no way to escape him.

As Maria and her father flew on to Texas where they would step into their new identities and begin to build their brand new life together, Dad and I flew back to San Jose. When we got home, we walked up the steps and found a notice taped to the front door. Dad tore it off and read it. "It's from Child Protective Services," he said. "They have Chrissy. Damn it!" He stormed inside cursing whoever had made that call and got on the phone demanding his daughter's immediate release. I was scared. I didn't know what Child Protective Services was or that they could just come and take Chrissy away. Dad slammed the phone down and turned to me. "They won't release Chrissy until they talk to you."

"Me? What do I have to do with Chrissy being taken, or with her coming back home?" I asked, confused.

"They want to know if Chrissy or you are being neglected by me. It appears that someone, they conveniently refuse to say who, but I'm guessing it's nosey neighbor Ruth, has made a complaint about neglect going on in our home. They want to know if it's true. That's why they want to talk to you."

I shook my head. "No. I don't want to talk to them. I don't even know what to say. What if I say the wrong thing, Dad, and they take me away, too?" I asked, trembling.

"They can't do that if you tell them there's no neglect or abuse going on here, okay?"

"Well, okay, I'll go talk to them if I have to, but I'm still really scared."

"I know you are," he said, holding me tight. Of course he knew. He always knew how I felt. "Just remember, stay calm, pause a moment before you answer, and keep it simple. Always keep it simple."

"Simple?" I asked.

"Yes. Simple. The best answers are 'yes' or 'no'. If you have to say more to answer a question, keep it as short as you can. Don't try to explain anything."

I nodded.

"Oh, and one more thing, Lily..."

"What?" I asked, still shaking.

"I wouldn't say anything about our relationship if I were you. If anyone knew, you *would* be taken away from me."

"Oh, no, Dad, don't worry. I won't." I didn't want to be taken away from my dad. Now that I was back with my dad, I never wanted to lose him again.

The next day I sat trembling in a small room with a CPS caseworker trying to look calm and unconcerned like Dad always did. The truth was I had never been more scared in my life. I was terrified I would say or do the wrong thing and be taken away and thrown in some foster home somewhere, never to see my dad again. I was afraid Chrissy would be too. So, I made sure that each answer I gave was simple, like Dad had said. I wasn't a very good liar. How could I be? This was the first time I could remember lying. But I knew I had to. I guess I was a better liar than I thought, because the CPS officer believed me and let me and Chrissy go back with our dad.

Chrissy, now seven, was very confused. She wondered why she had gotten into so much trouble when all she had done was call Ruth to ask her how to cook a can of Franco American Spaghetti in the microwave because she was hungry? Chrissy couldn't understand why Ruth would report Dad to CPS. All Chrissy had wanted was some help. Dad had asked Eric to come by and check on Chrissy that day, but Eric had gotten busy with some other things and ran late. "A good neighbor would've come by to help a child make her lunch," Dad said, "not report her to CPS." As I held Chrissy on my lap, we all nodded in agreement. "That's it!" Dad said. "We're moving!"

Dad sold the Minx home and with the money he made bought a few acres in Quincy. To keep the land well hidden from his creditors,

Dad put the land in my name. He told me we would build our dream home on the land one day. I was thrilled and wanted to keep "our" property safe. Like Dad always said, anyone can sue you and get a judgment against you, but if you don't own assets like a house or a piece of property to put a lien on or have money like a paycheck to garnish, the person won't collect a dime from you. Dad said he wasn't going to pay Betty's medical bills or funeral costs, and no one would be able to collect a dime from him because he was self-employed with no paycheck to garnish and had no property in his name to put a lien on.

In August we moved fifteen miles away to a rental house on Rainfall Drive in Sunnyvale. Our new home was a nice, single-story, four-bedroom, two-bath house. I was so glad to leave the home that had been haunting me. One of the four bedrooms in our new rental home was my pretend room, the same setup as I had had before. Slowly, Dad's master bedroom began to feel like "ours" (unlike the previous one in the Minx house, which had always felt like Betty's too).

Sadly, the landlord didn't allow pets, so Dad got rid of Buddy. Dad said there was no choice. We had to move and this was the best rental he could find. When Connor got back from Southern California that September and found out Buddy was gone, he was heartbroken, and I felt so bad for him.

It felt strange to be back in my old neighborhood. Our new house on Rainfall Drive was right around the corner from Carlos's house. And just down the street from us was Redwood Apartments, the same apartment complex where I'd lived with Mom and from which I'd run away only seven short months before. I'd never wanted to come back here or anywhere near here again. And yet here I was.

It also felt strange to be back in my old high school—Copperfield High—where my dad had re-enrolled me. I didn't realize how much I had missed my old friends, especially Les, my very tall ex-neighbor with bright blond hair. We used to walk nearly four miles to and from school together every day, talking and laughing. I had missed his gentle temperament and quirky sense of humor. Back when we'd lived at the Redwood Apartments, Les and I made weekly excursions to the laundry room. I brought the pot of chili with two tablespoons, and he brought the gallon of milk. Together we slurped, chugalugged, chatted, and chuckled our way through the wash and dry cycles. It seemed like we always had fun no matter what we did. He could always make me laugh, and I was glad to have him back in my life.

One day after school, I introduced Les to my dad. Les was looking for a way to make some extra money, so Dad hired him to help us with surveillances. It was great to work with Les. When the stake-outs got long and boring, Les would act silly and make Dad and me laugh so hard we almost cried. Dad said when Les turned eighteen in a few months he could do some process serving too.

At the end of the day, I looked forward to cuddling up to my dad and falling asleep in his arms. I celebrated my seventeenth birthday with Dad, Les, Connor, and Chrissy. When I blew out the candles on my cake, my only wish was that Dad and I would always be this happy.

Our first Christmas together was celebrated in our new home. Every cent I made from work had gone into a shoebox hidden under a pile of clothes on the top shelf of the closet in my pretend room because I wanted to buy a twenty-four-karat gold chain I had seen in one of the jewelry stores in the mall. It cost two hundred and fifty dollars, which took me nearly three months to save up. But I didn't care. I knew it would look perfect hanging around my dad's neck, and I couldn't wait to see the look on his face when he opened up his gift.

We placed our first Christmas tree in front of the big bay window in the living room that faced the street, where it could be seen by us and others in our neighborhood. Dad brought out a big box of ornaments for us to decorate the tree. As I looked through the box, a pretty porcelain angel caught my eye. It had fluffy white wings, a long glistening gold robe, and a beautiful face with a hopeful expression. I carefully picked it up and placed it on an upper branch. "No, Lily," Chrissy said patiently, "Mommy always puts the angel on *top* of the tree." My heart sank. I'd had no idea. My mom had always put a star on top of our tree.

For everyone but me, this was the first Christmas without Betty. I looked over at Connor, who sat alone on the couch in the corner of the living room staring at the Christmas tree with tears welled up in his eyes, and for a fleeting instant I saw that our first Christmas together was anything but festive and merry. Instead, it was full of pain and immense sadness. But it was far too much for a seventeen-year-old girl like me to handle. So I didn't. I somehow managed to banish it all from my mind.

On Christmas morning, I couldn't wait to open Dad's present—a guitar of my very own. Next, Dad opened his present from me. "Thank you, Lily. I love it. I can't wait to wear it," he said. He was grinning from ear to ear. Then he reached over and wrapped me in a big bear hug. I got lost in Dad's warm embrace, all the while thinking this was the merriest Christmas ever. On the floor, I saw a content Chrissy playing with the new Barbie doll and Breyer horse she had gotten for Christmas while Connor quietly retreated to his room and closed the door.

One cold January morning, Dad and I were at his PI office working on the latest case when, unexpectedly, Dad's legal secretary Jill appeared at the office door with a sheriff, a short man with an enormous belly and nearly bald head. In his hand were papers. I slowly put the phone down and stared at the sheriff. A lot of people came in and out of Dad's office, but never a sheriff.

"The sheriff wants to talk to you, Bill," Jill said.

"Yes, Sheriff," Dad said in his serious business voice, "what can I do for you?"

"Yes, hello, Mr. Capello," the sheriff said, then glanced over at me and nodded. I nodded back. "I'm Deputy O'Donnell with the Santa Clara County Sheriff's Department," he said, flashing his badge. "I'm sorry to bother you on this fine morning, but the reason why I'm here is because I have a legal document for you, a Writ of Execution. It appears Darling and Fischer provided you with funeral services for, hmm, wait, let me see." The sheriff clumsily thumbed through the pages he was holding until his fat fingers found the part he was searching for. "Oh yes, here it is. It looks like it was for your wife, Betty Capello." The sheriff paused and looked at my dad seriously for a moment, then continued. "As you are fully aware, Mr. Capello, Darling and Fischer has a money judgment against you. And, Darling and Fischer's attorney has instructed me, the levying officer, to levy on your business to satisfy its money judgment. This means, Mr. Capello, sir, that I, as the Keeper, will stay here on your premises for the next eight hours, or the entire business day, and collect all money you make until the time paid for is up or until the judgment against you is collected." The sheriff handed Dad the Writ of Execution.

I knew my dad had not paid any of Betty's medical bills or funeral expenses and had no intention of doing so. There was only a small tag provided free by the cemetery that marked Betty's grave, my dad's deliberate way of showing she was not worthy of commemoration. But I couldn't understand how Dad could be so calm when the sheriff was about to do what Dad had said could never be done—force him to pay something he owed.

I stared at my dad, waiting to see what we were supposed to do next, and saw his expression change from stern to mildly amused. Dad looked up at the sheriff and said firmly, "Sheriff, I'm closing the office for the day." I continued to stare at my dad, wondering what he was doing.

"Okay, Mr. Capello," the sheriff said in a calm, matter-of-fact voice, "then it looks like I'll be unable to collect any money today." The sheriff waited as Dad told Jill it was her lucky day. She was free to go home.

"With pay, right Bill?" Jill asked. Dad nodded reluctantly.

Everyone took the elevator down to the ground floor and went their separate ways. Dad smiled and waved goodbye to the sheriff as if they were good friends. Jill thanked my dad for the day off with pay. Dad and I drove around the block. Then we returned to the office to get some work done.

Dad was flipping through the pages of a file when I heard him chuckle.

"What's so funny?" I asked, looking up from the stack of papers in front of me.

"Oh, I'm sure Darling and Fischer were expecting to collect some money from me today. Instead, all they got for their trouble was a hundred and fifty dollar sheriff bill." Dad chuckled again, quite amused. I nodded, but I didn't find it at all amusing. No matter how my dad had felt about Betty, not paying for her funeral seemed so wrong, but I didn't say anything. "This afternoon I'll consult with a bankruptcy attorney. Once I declare bankruptcy, none of my creditors will collect a dime. Not even a Sheriff Keeper will come out then." He grinned and went back to work.

In May, soon after I received my high school diploma, we were evicted from our house on Rainfall Drive because Dad hadn't paid the rent. I heard my dad on the phone with our landlord saying he was still waiting for a check from an attorney he had recently done some detective work for. Dad apologized profusely and said once the check arrived he would pay six months rent in advance along with the back rent he owed. He sounded so sincere, but then he hung up and laughed. Later, when the landlord called looking for the rent money Dad had promised him, Connor, Chrissy, and I knew to tell him that our dad had been called away on business and that he would pay the rent as soon as he got home. Dad said it was easy to live rent-free. You just had to know what to say and when to go. "Once you move into a rental," Dad said, "there's only *one* person who can move you out—the sheriff." The day before the sheriff came to evict us, we left. I had never been evicted before, but I thought it was exciting to be getting away with stuff like that.

It seemed simple enough to get our next rental house in South San Jose. Dad and Eric got together one afternoon and over a couple of beers went over the details of the plan. Dad would put Eric's name down as his previous landlord on the rental application. They decided on things like property location, rental cost, and rental dates. Eric would tell the potential new landlady that Dad was a caring, trustworthy, and kind forty-year-old Christian widower with three children. He was a loving and devoted father, a hardworking, self-employed private investigator. He made a good living, always paid his rent on time, and took very good care of the property, inside and out.

"I just have one question, Bill," Eric said. "If you were such a great tenant, why would you leave? Like, I'm not going to kick you out or anything."

"Good question, Eric. Let's go with a family emergency. I had to go back east to take care of my very sick mother," Dad said without a second's hesitation. I wondered how my dad could think up lies so easily.

"Yeah, that sounds good," Eric said. "And, of course, I had to rent out my property to some new tenants since I had no idea if or when you might be back in town. I hope your very sick mother feels better very soon, Bill." We all laughed. This was almost too easy.

Later that week I overheard Eric, aka our previous pretend landlord, on the phone with our soon-to-be new landlady. "Oh, I can promise you, you won't have any problems with Bill. He's such a good tenant." The landlady called Dad shortly after and offered us her rental property on Kipling Court. I never knew exactly what had happened, but after we moved to Kipling Court, I never saw Eric again.

In the fall of '78, after living in our latest rental for four-and-a-half months, we were evicted from our home because Dad hadn't paid the rent, again. Once again, the day before the sheriff came to evict us, we left. Our next rental, a single-story, four-bedroom, two-bath house on Mulberry Drive looked a lot like our rental on Rainfall Drive, except older. I was moving more than I had when I'd lived with my mom. I had now lived in four homes since moving in with my dad a little over a year and a half before.

Dad treated Connor badly. Without Betty around to cherish and spoil Connor anymore, Dad was free to treat him as he saw fit. Dad announced one afternoon that there would be no more trips to Hollister Hills SVRA and sold Connor's beloved motorcycle. This was Connor's punishment for misbehaving—not listening to Dad, talking back, and sneaking out at night. From then on, Dad basically ignored Connor. Dad even looked into sending Connor away. He called a military school and a camp for delinquent teens but stopped when he heard the cost, angry that it wasn't free. It wouldn't be until much later that I learned the real reason my dad mistreated Connor the way he had, and my heart would break for my brave little brother.

When Dad and I were home, which was rarely, he treated Chrissy lovingly. He talked, laughed, and joked around with her. At night, he enjoyed reading Chrissy bedtime stories before tucking her in, but he spent most of his time with me, both at home and away.

Whenever Dad and I were away on jobs or trips, Connor was

expected to watch Chrissy. Dad was neglecting them, spending all his time with me like we were a happily married couple without kids. After years of my mom's abusive treatment, I was so hungry for my dad's love and attention, I desperately soaked up every moment. And sadly, because I was so focused on my dad and my own needs, I was oblivious to Connor's and Chrissy's needs.

I shared with my dad that I had begged my mom for a dog, but she did not allow me to have my own dog, only a family pet which was chosen by her. Our latest rental home allowed dogs, so I was ecstatic when my dad allowed me to pick a puppy of my *very* own— a frisky, affectionate, and very adorable eight-week-old Labrador retriever. Dad and I were co-owners, with the agreement that I would do all the training and Dad would pay all the costs. We also agreed that since Dad was the adult with the money, his name should go first on her AKC paperwork for ownership. Like parents trying to choose the perfect baby name, we sat on the couch for hours tossing around possible puppy names. We chose her name carefully. I wanted "thirteen" as part of her name because that was my lucky number, and I felt like the luckiest kid in the world to have found her. Because she was black and sweet as candy, Dad and I decided to name her Black Gumdrop the Thirteenth.

Connor missed his dog Buddy. He really wanted to get another dog, but for reasons I didn't quite understand, Dad said no. Dad's saying no to Connor but yes to me crushed Connor and made our already strained relationship even worse. Every time he saw my dog he was reminded of how unfair it all was, which fueled his hatred toward me even more.

When Gumdrop was three months old, Dad and I took her to obedience school where she graduated top of her class. She was incredibility smart and picked up on things quickly, making it easy for me to train her. Next, Dad and I entered her in AKC obedience trials. I was her handler. Sometimes I felt nervous, but Dad came to every trial to watch and cheer us on. He was our biggest fan. In the ring, I felt more comfortable and confident knowing my dad was there. A few months later, Gumdrop earned an AKC Companion Dog (CD) title. Dad and I were so proud of her. Gumdrop was like our child, and she had just earned top honors.

One warm August morning, as I sat on the cool kitchen floor roughhousing with Gumdrop, Dad said I should call Mom. "You haven't called her in a very long time, Lily," he said. I hadn't spoken to her since that first call, almost a year and a half before.

I shrugged. "So? Why should I call her?"

"Because, you only have one mom...and she loves you," Dad said. I looked down at the tile floor and shook my head. "Yes, Lily, believe it or not, your mom *does* love you. And, you need to call her every once in a while to let her know you're okay."

"I don't want to call her, Dad."

"Why?"

"I don't have anything to say to her." Every time I thought about calling my mom my stomach hurt. Even though she was seven hundred miles away, it wasn't far enough. She still scared me. I was afraid she would be able to reach through the phone lines and somehow still hurt me.

"You could let her know how well you're doing. Talk about work, Gumdrop. Let her know how happy you are." I looked at him, upset. He looked right back and flashed me a dazzling smile that made my resistance melt away.

"Fine." I lit a cigarette, picked up the phone, and called my mom.

"Hello, Mom, it's me, Lily."

"Well, hello, Lily. It's nice to hear from you. It sure has been awhile. How have you been?"

"I'm doing fine. I've just been really busy, you know, working with my dad on all sorts of fun and exciting cases."

"Uh-huh," Mom said. I could feel my mom's disappointment but tried to ignore it.

"Like on this latest case, Dad and I tailed this sleazy married doctor to the EZ 8 Motel over on First Street, where he was cheating on his wife with his nurse. I got pictures and everything, Mom. It was so cool!"

"Uh-huh..." Mom mumbled.

"Oh, and Mom, I have this sweet black lab now. Her name's Gumdrop, and she's so cute and so smart. I just love her so much." Mom didn't say anything. When my words were met by her silence, I was crushed. *How mean*, I thought. *Why can't she just be happy for me?*

After a long pause, she finally said, "That's nice, Lily, and is everything else okay there?" It was like she wanted to hear how bad it was, that Dad was a horrible person, that she had been right all along. But that couldn't have been further from the truth.

"Everything's fine here, Mom," I said firmly. "How's everything there?"

"Good. Eileen and Bart are doing well, and you have a new little sister now. Her name's Cindy, and she's a very happy baby, just like Bart was."

"That's great."

"And, I just got married to a wonderful man named Pierre, and I'm very happy." Her words were met by my silence. I couldn't be happy for her. After all the hurt and damage she had done to me, I didn't care about her or her new husband.

"Whatever happened to Ned? Did you marry him, too?" I didn't really care what had happened to Ned, but I figured I should at least know if Pierre was her fourth or fifth husband.

"Yes, I did marry Ned, but we're divorced now. He wasn't a good husband, or father."

"Uh-huh..." I mumbled. Then I chuckled to myself at the thought of Elizabeth Taylor being the only person I could think of that had been married more times than my mom. I was pretty sure the movie star was married to her sixth husband, but she was eleven years older than my mom, so my mom still had plenty of time to catch up and beat Elizabeth's record for most husbands.

"Well, Lily, I'm glad that you called, and I want you to remember that I love you very, very much."

"Yeah, okay Mom," I said, but I didn't care if she loved me or not. I didn't even believe her.

"Before you hang up, would you like to talk to Eileen?"

"Sure."

Eileen got on the phone for a few minutes. She told me she missed me a lot. I told her I missed her too. Then she told me a little about school before we said our goodbyes. It was nice to hear her voice again.

After hanging up, I told my dad that my mom didn't care about me. She didn't sound at all interested in what I had to say. And since I didn't care about her either, there really was no point in calling her again.

But Dad didn't want to hear it. He said, "You only get one mom, Lily, and you need to call her." I rolled my eyes and walked away. At the time I thought my dad was pushing me to call my mom because he had loved her once and didn't want her to worry. But now I know he did it only to hurt her. He wanted my mom to never forget that she might have won the custody battle when I was seven, but she had lost the war because her daughter was now with her father. And there wasn't a damn thing she could do about it.

During the winter of 1978-79, Dad and I returned to the cabin in Tahoe often. It became one of our favorite hideaways. We took Gumdrop to Tahoe with us where she loved to eat snow while trying to run through it like a plow clearing a path for an automobile. When she got too exhausted to take another step or too full to take another bite, she would collapse in the snow and bark at it loudly. Dad and I would look at her, then at each other, and laugh. When we got too cold we'd retire inside, leaving Gumdrop outside to work out her issues with the snow.

In Tahoe, I took a picture of Dad and Gumdrop. Dad was kneeling in a thick layer of fresh, fluffy snow. He wore a white sweater fading into browns and reds and a little black beanie. The shiny gold chain I had gotten him for Christmas looked so beautiful hanging around his neck just like I knew it would. To his left sat Gumdrop with her ears up at attention, her back leg jetting out to the right and her black coat looking blacker than a moonless winter night against the bright white snow. It was the perfect snapshot—the person and animal I loved most in the world, surrounded by tall green pines with just a hint of blue sky peeking through the dark green needle clusters, our Tahoe secrets captured in Dad's happy grin and Gumdrop's playful eyes. I framed my favorite photo and placed it on the mantel at home. Sometimes when I walked by it, I swore I could hear Gumdrop barking loudly at the snow and Dad and I laughing loudly watching her.

Those times spent in Tahoe meant the world to me. Once we stepped through the cabin door we were real. We didn't have to pretend anymore. Dad was more than my parent—he was my lover and my best friend. And Gumdrop was more than our pet—she was like our child, possessing a boundless energy and a constant desire to please and play. She was such a wonderful addition to our secret family. I had never felt more alive or more loved than I did in Tahoe.

One time, I lay in the cozy cabin with my naked body sprawled across my dad's chest, happier than I had ever been. I was very delicately tracing the outline of his nipple with my fingers, watching it pucker and stiffen with desire and wondering why we had to keep our affair secret. And the more I wondered, the angrier I became. It just wasn't making any sense to me. Why would anyone care? No one seemed to care if I was getting beaten by my mom and terrified, but now they'd care if I was having sex with my dad and happy? Well, fuck them, then. Fuck them all! I didn't care if the whole world did hate me for having sex with my dad. I didn't care one bit! To me it was fun, natural, and felt really good. No, it felt really great.

My feelings for my dad didn't change overnight. But as sure as the Tahoe snow slowly melted away late that spring, I slowly began to fall out of love with my dad. I was eighteen, and we had been lovers for two years. I really couldn't understand why I was falling out of love with him. Lots of people fell in and out of love all the time, but not us. We were different. Ours was true love and it was supposed to last forever. Or so I believed back then.

Maybe all his criminal activity led up to my change in feelings. Or perhaps it was how easily he could lie, or leave Connor and Chrissy behind, sometimes even without food. Maybe it was me. I had changed. I wasn't sure. The only thing I was sure of was that he was starting to remind me of a weasel, like he had when we first reunited at Pat's house, and I didn't like it. I wanted my sweeter and cuter otter image back. I felt confused and angry. It wasn't supposed to be this way. But no matter how hard I tried to fight it, my feelings for my dad were changing. I desperately needed his love and support, but I didn't want to have sex with him anymore to get it.

One warm summer day in June, Dad and I sat at our favorite table by the window in the small sandwich shop across the street from his office. We ordered our usual sandwiches, Dad's club on wheat, my ham and Swiss on rye. I leaned over the table and blurted out, "Dad, I love you. I always will. You're the best dad in the whole world. But—"

"But what, Lily?" he stared at me as if he could see right through me. I hated when he looked at me that way. It made me feel naked and small and very vulnerable. I had to look away. I looked down at my sandwich and tore off a piece of the extra crispy crust, wondering how I could ever get my dad to understand how important this was to me, never thinking he probably already knew.

"But...but...I really, really want to go on a blind date. Please." There, I said it. I wasn't sure how he would take my request. Dad's legal secretary, Jill, had explained that she wanted to play matchmaker and introduce me to a wonderful guy she knew would be "perfect" for me. I wanted my dad's approval, or I wouldn't go on the date.

"I don't think that's a good idea," Dad said.

"Please, Dad, please, pretty please," I begged.

"Come on, why would you want to go on a blind date anyway? You know no one will ever love you more than your dad."

"Yeah, I know. But, I just want us to have a normal relationship, you know, like other dads and daughters do. I want us both to date other people." He glanced down and shook his head in disapproval. "Please, Dad," I insisted, "I really want to go on this blind date."

"Okay, if that's what you really want, then fine, go."

I couldn't believe it. My dad had said yes. I felt so happy, but when I saw his big, sad eyes, I felt sad too.

"Promise you won't be mad at me, even if we don't have sex anymore?" It wasn't like we were having much sex lately anyway. We hadn't had sex in almost two months, whereas we used to have sex almost every day.

"Promise," he said.

"Promise you'll still love me, always?" I asked, sure that there must be a catch.

"Yes, you'll always be my 'lovey-dove,'" my dad said, reassuring me.

"I love you Dad—you're the best." I got up from the table and gave him a big hug and kiss on the cheek.

"Oh, just one more thing, Lily," he said as we exited the shop. *Oh great*, I thought, *here comes the catch.*

"What?"

"Since it'll be too difficult for me to watch you go on this blind date, knowing you will be with another man, I'll be taking a trip to

Tahoe that night. I hope you understand," he said as we crossed San Pedro Street on our way back to the office.

"Yes, I understand. I know it's hard. It'll be hard for me, too, you know, when you start dating," I said with tears in my eyes. Still, I couldn't wait to get back to the office and tell Jill the good news: Yes, I'd be able to make the blind date this weekend.

That night Dad said it would be best if my pretend room now became my real room since I wanted to date now. I agreed, although I really didn't like lying there alone in my cold bed. I had slept in Dad's warm bed for over two years. I didn't want to have sex with him; I just wanted to lie next to him and talk like we always had. More than anything, I wanted a father, not a lover.

I stared out my bedroom window and fantasized about what my "perfect" blind date would be like, what he would look like. Was it going to be love at first sight, complete with fireworks exploding all around us like it was on TV? The plan was to go over to Jill's house, where Sam and I would meet, and then have dinner with Jill and her fiancé Matt. Jill told me how sweet Sam was, and that she had a good feeling that the two of us would hit it off. I trusted Jill and her judgment, so I was eager to meet my blind date.

The next morning Dad didn't have much to say to me. Instead of joining me for breakfast like he usually did, he left without saying goodbye. At the office, he joked around with Jill but basically ignored me. Then he told Jill how happy he was that I was finally getting out and dating and thanked her for setting me up on this blind date. I thanked Jill too and smiled at my dad, but he looked away. I was worried that he was mad at me for going on the blind date, and part of me felt sad that our relationship had to change. But I wanted to go and wanted my dad to know it, so I told Jill excitedly that I couldn't wait to meet Sam that weekend. Without a word or look in my direction, Dad turned and left the office. I didn't see him for the rest of the day. For the next two days, he continued his cold treatment, hardly speaking to me, ignoring me like he hated me, like I wasn't even his daughter anymore.

As I drove my new '79 Daytona blue Mazda RX-7 (that I, not Dad, had paid for) to Jill's Santa Cruz beach home, I was on cloud nine. I was aching for a good time with a boy my own age, and the possibilities greatly intrigued me. Still, part of me missed my dad, and I couldn't stop thinking about him. I wondered if he was packing for his trip to Tahoe, once our favorite hideaway. Did he miss me like I missed him? I nervously knocked on the door, pushing all thoughts of my dad out of my mind. Jill ushered me into the kitchen where she introduced me to Sam. "Hello, nice to meet you, Lily. I've heard a lot about you," Sam said, smiling.

"Yeah, nice to meet you, too, Sam, and I've heard a lot about you, too," I said as I glanced over at a smiling Jill. Unfortunately, what I had heard and what I saw in front of me didn't match. He was nothing like I had imagined. He was not cute as Jill had indicated. He was short, barely as tall as I was, a bleached blond with a small but wiry figure, average looking, and definitely nothing out of the ordinary in his Hawaiian print shirt, board shorts, and flip flops. He did have a nice tan though. *Okay*, I thought, *maybe once I get to know him, I will see in him what Jill sees in him.* Surely he had wonderful qualities for me to discover, and I would be pleasantly surprised. I told myself to keep an open mind.

While Jill prepared enchiladas and put some guacamole and chips on the kitchen table, Matt, a larger, cuter, and far sexier version of Sam, came around with a pitcher. "Would either of you like a drink?" Matt asked Sam and me. "I make a mean margarita."

"Yeah, thanks Matt," I replied as I munched on a tortilla chip. He handed me a glass and I took a sip. Matt was right, his margaritas were mean and strong.

"Awesome. Thanks, brah," Sam said.

After dinner, Sam and I went for a walk. We made our way down the worn and steep cliff stairs and then climbed down many slippery rocks to get to Pleasure Point beach.

"Have you been to this beach before?" Sam asked.

"No, I haven't. Have you?" I asked.

"Yep, I was just here this morning, surfing with my buddies," he said as he gazed longingly at the waves. "It was epic. There are some awesome surf spots here like Sewers, First Peak, and Little Wind and Sea. Do you surf, too?"

"No, I don't."

"Well, have you ever wanted to?" he asked eagerly.

"No, I prefer to watch."

"There's a lot to surfing, you know," Sam said excitedly.

"Really?" I said, trying to look interested.

"Oh, yeah..." He droned on and on about the ocean, the waves, the techniques, the maneuvers, the competitions, the tricks, his surfboard, his surf buddies ... blah, blah, and blah. He bored me stiff with detailed explanations ranging from how to perfectly wax and polish a surfboard to how the winds, tides, and bathymetry played crucial roles in surfing. *Is this guy for real?* I thought. *I wish he would go and catch a perfectly gnarly wave, like now! Does he ever come up for air? Does he ever get tired of hearing himself speak? Will he ever stop talking long enough to notice that I'm walking right alongside him on this freaking beach too? Geez, this sucks.* As I tuned out Surfer Sam's self-absorbed, boring babble, I tuned in to the self-talk radio broadcasting in my head. *What in the world am I doing here? I blew off my dad for this? Am I crazy?* I really, really missed my dad. I would have given anything to have been with my dad right then, heading off to Tahoe and having fun. I needed to find him and talk to him. I wanted to pretend this blind date from hell had never happened and go back to the way things had been before.

At that time, the thought of losing my dad was a fear worse than any I'd ever known. I didn't want him mad at me, ignoring me. I didn't want to be in my pretend room, lying alone in my bed.

Instead, I wanted to be back in my dad's bed, safe again, wrapped in his protective, loving arms. I wanted to laugh, talk, and have fun together like we used to. I really did believe that I would die if I didn't have my dad in my life.

I was ready to admit to my dad as soon as I got home that I had made a huge mistake and should never have gone on that blind date. I wanted to offer my sincere apologies, kiss, make up, and have our relationship back to the way it was. But when I got home, the house was empty. Dad was already gone. I was too late. My worst nightmare had come true: I had been abandoned. I would have done anything to find my dad and get back in his favor. Panic-stricken, I phoned every casino in Tahoe and had my dad paged at every establishment. My heart sank a little lower each time an operator came back on the line to say, "I'm sorry Ma'am, but Bill is not answering the page."

With nowhere left to call, unable to ask my dad for his forgiveness, I lost it. I stood in the middle of the living room floor staring at the Tahoe photo on the mantel and began howling at the top of my lungs like a wounded animal who needs to be shot and put out of her misery. I screamed out for my dad. Dropping to my knees, I pounded my fists into the ugly green carpet until the bones in my hands hurt. I huddled against the wall in the corner, weeping, while Gumdrop howled loudly in the backyard. Thankfully Connor and Chrissy were spending the night at friends' houses.

I hated myself for being stupid enough to actually believe that another guy could replace or even come close to my dad, the person I loved more than anyone else in the whole world. I realized my dad was right—no one would ever love me like he loved me, and I had to wonder if he still did. I feared I had lost my dad forever. Without him I was completely alone. I cursed myself a thousand times for going on that damn blind date. Delirious and exhausted, I curled up in the fetal position and cried myself to sleep.

Ring ring. Ring ring. I quickly jumped up and made a mad dash to answer the phone. It was my dad, his voice like a lifeline. I began crying and apologizing for going on the blind date, then pleading with him to please tell me where he was so I could meet him there.

"Now, come on, you were the one who begged me to let you go on the blind date, and I let you go. I don't think you should be with me now just because the date didn't work out. Besides, I am not going to be your last resort until something better comes along. Sorry," he clearly proclaimed.

"Dad, please! I'm so sorry. I promise I'll never go on another date again, ever. I love you, and I only want to be with you. I miss you. Please, just tell me where you are, okay?"

There was a long pause and I feared he would hang up at any moment. "Okay, fine. If it's that important to you, and you really want to drive all the way up here just to be with your dear old dad, and you promise no more dating, then I guess I'll tell you where I am," he said teasingly.

"Yes, I really want to be with you, and like I already said, I promise no more dating. So please tell me where you're staying."

"Okay, I'm in Carson City staying at the Ormsby House."

I couldn't get to Carson City fast enough. As I drove, I felt on top of the world, knowing I would soon be back with my dad, the one person who loved and understood me completely.

Arriving breathless at his hotel door, I knocked and waited, and waited some more. After what seemed like an eternity, my dad finally opened the door. I immediately jumped into his arms and kissed him.

I was only eighteen; however, with a fake ID in hand, gambling and drinking were instantly legal. My dad taught me how to play craps, but blackjack quickly became my all-time favorite casino game as I easily turned twenty dollars worth of casino chips into one hundred dollars—time and time again. My dad called it beginner's luck; I jokingly called it skill. Good food and drinks, lots of fun, gambling, and sex were ours for the taking.

———

My first attempt at leaving my dad to date another man had been a complete bust, and for a long time afterward, whenever I did happen to meet a potential boyfriend, I would ask myself if it would be worth losing my dad and our relationship, and in the process upsetting him enough that I could possibly even lose, as in bitter divorce battles, my home, job, and family. Each time, after weighing all the pros and cons, I decided to stay with my dad, for the cost of leaving was potentially far too great. The scales always appeared to tip in my dad's favor, so I abandoned the idea of any interaction with other men. Often I felt frustrated, angry, and trapped, but my only option was to continue having sex with my dad so that I could keep our relationship stable and keep him in my life.

Chapter 7
ANTHONY

For the next two years, I buried myself in work, taking on as many jobs as possible. I was still doing my court run and running errands for attorneys during the day, but I was eighteen now and could serve legal documents too. Dad said I should never go out alone, so at night I took Chrissy along with me as I drove around town serving my latest stack of subpoenas, summonses, judgments, and divorce papers. Dad and I rarely had time to work on cases together anymore. We saw less and less of each other, but we still somehow managed to continue our sexual relationship and still found time to talk and have some fun together. We continued to go to concerts, Golfland, Tahoe, and Shasta, but it wasn't the same. Even though Dad was still acting like my lover and best friend, I didn't love him the way I used to.

Time flew by. A few weeks before I turned twenty-one, I finished my court run early and rushed home to watch my favorite soap opera, *General Hospital*. I was sitting on the couch fantasizing that sexy bad boy Luke Spencer was now my lover, when suddenly the phone rang. It was Eileen. She said she had had it with Mom. She was tired of Mom's yelling and beatings. She wanted to run away like

I had.

I explained the situation to Dad, and a week later Eileen moved in with us. It felt nice to be able to help my little sister out and to introduce her to my "other" family.

Eileen couldn't stop talking about her eighteen-year-old boyfriend Todd, an Idahoan native. They were in love and planned to marry the next year when Eileen turned sixteen. Seeing her so excited about Todd made me wish I had a normal boyfriend too. I fantasized about having a boyfriend my own age and a Dad who loved me even if we no longer had sex.

It was hard to believe it had been nearly five years since Dad and I started our affair, and I had never told anyone. Who was I going to tell? Connor and I didn't even like each other, and I felt more like Chrissy's mom than sister. But now Eileen was here. We shared a past history with our mom, and even though five years separated us, we seemed to have a lot in common. Sometimes I felt like I was exploding inside, and I wanted so desperately to talk to someone about my complicated relationship with my dad. Maybe I could trust Eileen; maybe she was the one person who could understand me, who wouldn't judge me, who would just listen. One night as we sat on my bed talking, I almost told her, but then I remembered the two times I'd shared a secret before.

When I was twelve years old, my best friend Kelly, also twelve, started the game. "Truth or Dare?" Kelly asked as she brushed an annoying strand of long, wavy red hair away from her freckled face. I had never played the game before, but Kelly promised me it would be fun.

"Truth," I said, guessing it would be easier to answer a question than to perform a dare.

"Okay, Lily, have you *ever* had sex?" she asked, waiting patiently but eagerly for my reply.

I looked at her, embarrassed, and said anxiously as I toyed with my hands, which rested in my lap, "Uh...yes." I paused. "Okay, my turn, truth or dare?" I asked.

"Truth," Kelly replied.

"Okay, then, same question to you. Have you ever had sex?"

"Yes." (I later found out that she was having sex with a sixteen-year-old neighbor boy.)

Then we played round two of Truth or Dare. I chose Truth. "So, *who* did you have sex with?" Kelly asked.

Shit, I didn't think this game was fun anymore. I had never told anyone and wasn't sure if I wanted to. "Kelly, do you *swear* on your life, that you will never, *ever*, tell anyone, *ever?*" I asked as I wondered if I could trust her.

"Swear! Cross my heart," Kelly said as she made an X over her heart with her finger, "and hope to die." I believed her.

"Carlos...my stepdad." I couldn't believe I had actually done it—I had said it, out loud. Big-eyed Kelly looked at me, shocked.

"Did you *like* having sex with your stepdad?"

"Eww! No, he's old and *gross!*"

"Then, why did you have sex with him? Is it still going on?"

I looked down at the floor. "Yeah."

"Does your mom know?"

"No."

"Why don't you just tell her?"

"I can't tell my mom. When Carlos first touched me almost a year ago, I was too scared to tell her. But he didn't touch me again...until a few weeks ago. Now he touches me and does stuff to me all the time. I hate it! I want to tell my mom so he'll stop, but I can't now. Not now. A few weeks ago, she tried to kill herself, so the police took her to El Camino Mental Hospital. Have you ever been to a mental hospital before, Kelly?"

Kelly shook her head. "No, I haven't."

"Well, I have, and I can tell you that it's the *scariest* place you'll ever go." I took a deep breath and continued. "I stood in front of a locked door. After being buzzed in, I walked down a long hallway. I saw people in there that looked like they were there, but they weren't."

"What? Where were they then?" she asked, bewildered.

"I don't know where they were, but I think it was somewhere far, far away. They didn't walk; they sort of shuffled. None of them talked or laughed or smiled. I don't think they could. Their faces had no expressions. But the most scariest thing of all was their eyes. Their eyes were totally empty."

"Empty?" Kelly asked, trying to picture what I was saying.

"Yeah, empty. Not sad or happy, just empty. Blank. Not real. Oh, wait. Look! Look Kelly! Look! Over there!" I said excitedly as I pointed to Kelly's dirty Raggedy Ann doll with her black button eyes that I spotted in the corner of her room. "They looked just like that!"

"Wow, that's creepy," Kelly said as she lit two cigarettes and handed me one. I puffed on it like an adult would, but careful not to inhale too deeply.

"Yeah, it is. And my mom just got released and is finally back home. Carlos said if I tell my mom, I would *destroy* her—I would send her right back to the mental ward. It would be *all* my fault," I said, in a panic. "I don't want my mom to go back to that scary place, *ever*, so I don't tell my mom about having sex with Carlos. Plus if my mom did go back then it would just be me and Carlos—*totally gross.*"

I trusted Kelly and told her everything because she swore on her life that she would never ever utter a word to another living soul. Well, she lied! The news spread like wildfire and before long I was teased and humiliated by classmates and even by kids I didn't know, but at least my mom didn't hear the news. I swore to myself I would *never* make that mistake again.

Then one summer, when I was still living with my mom and Carlos, my cousin Marla came to live with us. Marla's mom was Carlos's sister.

Marla and I were both fifteen. She had big dark eyes, long dark thick hair, and a perfect complexion. She liked to forget her problems by dropping acid. I told her she was crazy to take drugs that play tricks on your eyes, but she said it was really fun.

One night Marla asked me, "Does your dad look at you in a sexual way?"

I hesitated answering. I had trusted Kelly and shouldn't have. I didn't want to make the same mistake again. "I don't know, does your dad?"

Marla answered sheepishly, "Yes."

I nodded my head in agreement, "Yes, my dad does too." The back-and-forth questioning continued through the night.

"Does your dad lift up your shirt and feel your breasts?" Marla asked.

I replied, "I don't know, does your dad?"

"Yes."

"Yes, my dad does too."

"Does your dad have sex with you?"

"I don't know, does your dad?"

"Yes."

"Yes, my dad does too."

I trusted that our private cousin-to-cousin, heart-to-heart was for our ears only. I assumed it was a pretty safe bet Marla wouldn't tell anyone about Carlos and me like Kelly had since Marla's dad was doing the same sexual stuff to her too. Imagine my surprise when Marla not only told her mom about her dad's sexual games but then decided to tell about Carlos's too. Marla's mom immediately phoned my mom and told her. In the end, my mom did divorce Carlos, but I no longer trusted people to keep secrets.

Reflecting on how hurt and betrayed I felt when Kelly and Marla had told my secret, I decided not to share my secret with my sister. I feared Eileen would tell someone and I would lose everything. When she asked if I had a boyfriend too, I lied. Too scared to tell her my boyfriend since I was sixteen was my dad, I said I'd had one but we recently broke up. As much as I wanted to, I knew better than to share a secret like that with her or anyone else.

Eileen's boyfriend Todd came out to California a week after she had moved in with us. The two of them soon found a place of their own. They seemed very happy together. I was happy for her but sad for myself. I didn't see a way out of my relationship with my dad without losing everything.

I had never met anyone who was worth potentially losing everything for—my dad, my home, my family, my career—until Anthony.

Dad and I were on a bowling league at Oak Tree Lanes. We had a lot of fun competing against other teams. Anthony, a tall, dark, sexy Italian with a full beard and big brown eyes, was a bowler on an opposing team. Anthony and I were extremely competitive, focused on our games and bowling our darnedest. When Anthony's High Rollers team beat my Right On team, I secretly despised him, his endless strikes, and his incredibly high 193 bowling average. I contemplated accidently spilling a few drops of sticky soda where he normally stood waiting to bowl—definitely unsportsmanlike conduct, or "unsportswomanlike" conduct. There was no love lost between us at first. Then the strangest thing happened: the dislike began to magically melt away, and butterflies began to multiply and flutter wildly in my stomach whenever Anthony was near.

Anthony and I would chat as we waited for our teammates to bowl, and he was clearly interested in me. Sometimes when I got up to bowl I would see Anthony from across the lanes smiling at me. I always smiled back. I could feel the sparks between us. But Dad always hovered over me, which made it difficult for shy Anthony to find the right moment to ask me out.

Not wanting to piss my dad off, I didn't say a word about Anthony. But part of me wondered if he already knew how I felt. Could he feel the butterflies in my stomach too? I cringed at the thought.

For my twenty-first birthday my dad took me to Vegas to see my all-time favorite entertainer—master magician and illusionist Doug Henning. Seated in the front row, I watched in awe as this happy Canadian hippie with his long shaggy mane of hair and bushy mustache stepped out on stage in a bright orange outfit. He deftly sawed two women in half and reassembled them on each other's legs, escaped from a chained trunk like Houdini, and conjured up a Bengal tiger out of thin air. I watched every mind-blowing detail up-close, thinking I could catch a glimpse of how he did what he did. But I didn't.

The show may have temporarily quieted the butterflies, but they soon returned. That night, I couldn't stop thinking about Anthony; I felt like a lovesick puppy as I anxiously awaited our return home. Dad pulled me close to him and tried to kiss me. I pushed away. It was the first time I had ever pushed him away. "Damn it, Dad! Stop it! I don't like having sex with you anymore. Okay? I wish I did. But I don't." We lay in the hotel room surrounded by an awkward silence. Finally, I spoke. "It's not like I can just break up with you, just walk away and never see you again like I would an ex-boyfriend. You're my father. I need you. So, what the fuck am I supposed to do? Keep having sex with you, even if I hate it? Would that really make you happy, Dad?"

"No, Lily, that would not make me happy. And I wouldn't want you to do that. Like I've said before, I never want you to do *anything* you don't want to do." As I started to cry, feeling torn and confused, Dad pulled me back into his arms, his chest against mine. All the while I wondered what it might feel like to be wrapped in Anthony's arms.

"But if I don't have sex with you anymore, will you leave me? You know, I'd rather stay and have sex with you than have you leave me." It sounded so weak and wrong to say out loud, but that's what I truly felt.

"How can I leave you? I'm your father, and I always will be. I will always be here for you." He held me and slowly stroked my hair, wiping my tears and making it all better.

On the drive home Dad said he wanted me to date, feeling it would be good for my health and well-being. I know it sounds strange, but the more he wanted me to date, the more I didn't want to. I worried he was pushing me away, abandoning me when I needed him most. It felt like my insides were being ripped apart. I told him how much it hurt. Dad promised he'd never abandon me, even if we stopped having sex and even if I started dating, but I wasn't sure if I could believe him or not.

"I swear to God, Dad, if you leave me, I'll kill myself! I will!"

"Come on now, stop talking that way. You're stronger than you think you are."

"No, Dad. I'm really not." I remembered very clearly what had happened the last time I went on a date.

When we got home that night, Dad made it easy for me to stop having sex with him. He said I should sleep in my pretend room, which I reluctantly did. For the first time in almost two and a half years, since the three nights before the awful blind date, I slept alone in my cold bed.

The next day Dad took off without saying a word to anyone about where he was going. Chrissy and Connor didn't seem too bothered by it. They were used to Dad leaving them behind. I wasn't. Dad usually took me with him or, if I had work to do on my own, he always let me know where he was going.

That night I cried my heart out. Despite what my dad had said, he had abandoned me.

Two days later, Dad came wandering through the front door with a duffle bag, his rifle, and a smile. I immediately ran over to where he stood and began punching him as hard as I could as I yelled, "Where the hell have you been? How could you just leave like that without telling me where you were going? And after you'd promised me you'd never leave me! I hate you!"

Dad dropped his stuff and grabbed my hands to stop me from hitting him. "Hey, come on now, calm down. I just went out hunting with the boys for the weekend, no big deal. And after our last discussion, I thought you could use a little time to yourself. Besides, I knew you wouldn't want to go out and kill animals, now would you, Lily?" he asked as I began to cry. Then Dad hugged me, and in that moment all I wanted was him. We went upstairs to his bedroom where we had make-up sex.

Afterward everything went back to normal, Dad and me working and playing and sleeping together as if nothing had ever happened. Dad still said my dating was a good idea, and I still thought about Anthony, but I didn't want Dad to take off again and leave me. It hurt too much. Besides, I began to think I would never be strong enough to leave my dad anyway, so why bother trying.

About two months later, a dear friend and bowling teammate Gloria invited Anthony and me over to her house for coffee. Gloria was a sweet ex-hippie who had named our bowling team after her favorite phrase, "Right On," which she said often. She believed in peace, love, and the power of marijuana. Gloria thought Anthony and I hadn't gotten together yet because my dad was an overprotective parent, and she wanted to help us out. She invited me over for coffee, which was okayed by my dad. (Dad was always either with me or, if not, wanted to know where I was.) But what Dad didn't know was that Gloria had also invited Anthony. Gloria had no idea how much she had helped. At the bowling alley I had to keep my feelings about Anthony to myself. After all, Dad and I were still together and still having sex. But at Gloria's house I didn't have to hide my feelings. I finally had the chance to sit down without Dad there and really talk to Anthony instead of watching Anthony from afar or keeping the talk strictly to bowling to appease my dad.

Anthony and I sat next to each other on the couch, smiling nervously. "You two just need to relax a little," Gloria said as she lit a joint and offered us a hit. Anthony and I passed on the marijuana, but later when Gloria politely offered us some beer, we both said yes. "Right on!" Gloria smiled as she inhaled deeply, holding the joint. "Alcohol's good too." As we drank, Anthony told me about his family road trip from Staten Island to San Jose a few years before, and I told him about my PI work. The three of us also swapped bowling stories.

After having an incredibly pleasant evening, Anthony and I said good night to Gloria, who was thrilled to have gotten us together, and continued to chat in my car. The conversation flowed freely for hours; it was as if we had known each other forever. Suddenly, I saw my dad's truck pull up next to us and my heart sank. Dad got out of his truck, walked over, and saw us together in my car. He stood there for a moment, staring at me. Then, without saying a word, he got back into his truck and peeled off down the dark road, tires screeching.

I knew my dad was furious with me. I could tell by the look on his face. He had looked at me as if he wanted to kill me. I had never seen my dad look at me with such hatred before, the way my mom had just before she was going to hit me, and it scared me. In that instant I knew he hadn't meant it when he said I should date. Too afraid to go home, I told Anthony I was going to stay in a hotel for a few days until my dad cooled off. Anthony didn't ask me any questions, so I didn't have to explain anything. Not wanting me to be alone, he offered to stay with me. I smiled and happily accepted.

To make it more difficult for my PI dad to find me, I selected a hotel in another county, and checked in under a false name at a hotel in San Francisco. This would not only give Dad time to cool off, but also give Anthony and me the opportunity to get to know each other better away from Dad's watchful and jealous eye.

We spent four days in San Francisco. We talked and laughed and joked around like we were best friends who had known each other for years. It was all so easy and carefree. The more I got to know Anthony, the more I fell madly in love with him. I found out he had butterflies in his stomach too. And he had missed me as much as I had missed him when I had gone to Vegas with Dad. He said he had never met anyone like me before and couldn't stop thinking about me. We kissed and cuddled.

It had been five years since I had sex with anyone other than my dad, and I couldn't wait to go to bed with Anthony. But he didn't want to, not yet. He felt it was too soon and wanted us to take it slowly. The idea of waiting to have sex with him drove me absolutely crazy. Here we were in a hotel together far away from Dad, and I wanted Anthony. But I tried to respect his wishes. I really did. I waited the first night, and then the second, but by the third night, our last night alone together in the hotel, I couldn't take it any longer—*I* made love to *him*. It was wonderful. We were lying next to each other naked and sweaty when he wrapped his arms around me and said, "I love you, Lily." In that moment I knew he was worth risking it all for.

The next day, I drove back to San Jose with my hands trembling on the steering wheel, Anthony sitting next to me. I had no idea what to expect from my dad. Anthony wanted to go and talk with my dad, who he believed was just being an overprotective father. I told him no, please don't, because I wasn't going home anyway. I had no idea what my dad would say to Anthony.

I dropped Anthony off at his car, which was parked around the corner from Gloria's house, and promised to call him later. With nowhere else to go, I drove back to where it had all started, Gloria's house. Gloria told me that while Anthony and I were gone, Dad had gone to Oak Tree Lanes and told everyone there that Anthony and I had run off and he was very upset, angry, and worried. I asked Gloria if I could stay at her house for a little while until I decided what to do. She said, "Lily, of course you can. Stay as long as you need." While I was there, I didn't go back to work or call Dad. I felt confused and didn't know what I was going to do next.

At the end of the week, Dad sent me a letter.

> *My Dearest Daughter,*
>
> *As you are aware we are getting to know each other in a different way and we are slowly and tenderly drifting our separate ways. I know it is not easy to change. It's the hardest thing in your life to handle. But I know and you know that it's for the best, maybe not at the present, but the future is what's most important.*
>
> *As I've been telling you change is also good for your health, mental as well as physical. If you change your feelings and you feel good then that's what's important. And it really feels good if when you change your feelings, it makes someone else happy.*
>
> *Well as the days go on it will be trying, and sometimes difficult to talk. But remember somewhere, somehow and always I'll be there to listen, and most of all care.*
>
> *Lily, I love you more than anyone else in the Universe. As your dad I will not <u>desert</u> you and let you drift for yourself in this lonely and sometimes miserable society. I know you will need me at some time and I will be there to care, listen, and most of all love.*
>
> *Always keep this letter so you can remind yourself and me. You can always call me at 727-1611 or 923-8754 and find me.*
>
> *In closing, we have a special relationship, let's never lose it in such a way we will both be sorry. You're my only daughter who is a friend too. I know you so well that I get scared. Please try to keep your head up and do things that you will not be ashamed of to tell your children. I pray you will try to make me a proud Father and I can always say to my family and friends, that's my daughter Lily and she sure is the sharpest and smartest of my kids – I hope Chrissy and*

Connor turn out half as good.
Yours Always,
Dad
PS <u>*Think Positive.*</u>

My heart melted as I read my dad's letter. It sounded like Dad really did want to have a "normal" relationship too. But I was scared. I didn't know where my new relationship with Anthony would lead, and I didn't want to end up alone. The one thing I did know was that I loved my dad very much, and I wanted to work things out. I wanted my dad to always be in my life. I called and told Dad I was going to date Anthony. Dad said okay and reminded me that he had been the one who had encouraged me to date. I reminded him of his letter and his promise to never desert me and to always love me. He said, "Yes, Lily, I haven't forgotten." So after staying at Gloria's for a week, I returned home.

My dad was a cunning creature. He knew how I felt—abandoned and alone—and in his letter articulated my feelings for me not in a fatherly way, but instead in the way a person would whose sole purpose was to reel his victim right back in.

Dad said I should move into my pretend room for good, which I did. That night, I walked by Chrissy's bedroom and saw Dad lying next to eleven-year-old Chrissy in her bed, both of them under the covers fast asleep. Shocked, I stood there frozen in her doorway. The thought of my dad touching Chrissy sexually made me so mad that I felt like I could strangle him with my bare hands if I found out that he had. But wait, Dad wouldn't touch Chrissy, I reasoned. She was just a kid. There had to be some other explanation. Maybe Chrissy had had a nightmare, was too scared to sleep alone, and begged Dad to sleep with her. Or maybe they had stayed up late talking and had fallen asleep. But I couldn't forget what I'd seen, and I had to find out if anything had happened to Chrissy that night.

The following morning I confronted Dad in his bedroom, once "our" bedroom. "I saw you sleeping with Chrissy last night. You weren't touching her or anything, were you?" He looked at me and laughed, which really pissed me off because it was no laughing matter. "Dad, stop it! I'm being serious. Tell me, did you touch her? Did you have sex with her?" I asked, staring at him with disgust. Dad, seeing that I was being completely serious, looked down and shook his head like he was just as disgusted with me for thinking such a terrible thing. Then he took my hand and led me to the living room where Chrissy sat on the floor watching TV.

I stood next to Dad. Chrissy looked up from the TV, concerned. "Lily thinks we're having sex," Dad said in his very calm, matter-of-fact manner. "Chrissy, have I ever had sex with you or ever touched you inappropriately?"

Chrissy shook her head and shouted, "No. Never!" Chrissy looked just as disgusted and sickened by the thought as I did. Then she went back to watching the rest of her TV show. So I believed her. Why shouldn't I? She was very convincing.

Anthony and I continued to date, and Dad seemed to be fine with it. However, his true emotions occasionally peeked through his smooth but cracked façade. Dad started to give Anthony the cold shoulder, ignoring him when he came over to the house. Not understanding why my dad had taken such a dislike to him, Anthony blamed himself.

I wanted Dad to get to know Anthony, to sit down and talk with Anthony and give him a chance, so after we'd been dating for about a month, I asked my dad if I could invite Anthony over for dinner. My dad said yes, on one condition: I had to have sex with him one last time. Figuring it was the path of least resistance, and desperately wanting my dad to create a warm and friendly atmosphere, I reluctantly agreed. I hated every second, looking away as he entered me, hoping he would ejaculate soon so it would be over.

Afterward the foolish, immature questions began. "So, does Anthony have a bigger dick than me? Is that it?"

"Yeah, that's it. How'd you know?" I said. Angry, I continued to look away from him, focusing instead on the faded white paint and old crown molding on the bedroom walls as I wished my every word would slash like a knife blade into his flesh. I decided if he pushed me any further, I would tell him how truly small his stupid little worthless dick was, in hopes it would shrivel up and die—literally.

"Tell me, Lily, what can Anthony possibly offer you that I can't?"

"I don't know, Dad," I responded as I looked over at my record player atop his dresser with my Kiss album still on the turntable. I was so tired of his questions and of him. The last ounce of respect I had for my dad went right out the bedroom window when I caught this glimpse of his true colors—his once kind, warm, and loving behavior had become cold and cruel. His smiles had become malicious, his voice venomous.

"You know no one will ever love you more than your dad," Dad said knowingly.

"Yeah, Dad, I know," I said, but now I began to feel doubt creep in.

My dad did keep his word, though. He invited Anthony over for dinner and was on his best behavior as he made Anthony feel welcome and part of the family.

However, my dad's pretend "niceness" toward Anthony was short-lived. The following Saturday I was standing at the kitchen sink washing dishes when I heard a quick *click* followed by a louder frightening *clunk* behind me. I dropped the dish I was holding and quickly turned to see my dad holding a long slender rifle. He smiled at me and announced he was off to do some work. "Really?" I asked. "Work? What's with the rifle?"

"Oh, I thought I might drive by Anthony's house, and if I happen to see him close to his front window, I'd enjoy some target practice," he said with a devilish smirk that was growing bigger by the second.

"Yeah, right Dad. Quit joking around. That's not funny," I said, shaking my head.

"Who said I was joking?" He was grinning from ear to ear pointing the rifle at the kitchen window, his left eye staring through the rifle scope and his right index finger on the trigger as if he were aiming and shooting at Anthony.

"Whatever you say. Have fun at work. Bye," I said dismissively. I turned and went back to washing dishes, ignoring Dad.

"Okay, I'm leaving, but before I go you might want to call Anthony and warn him not to stand *too* close to his front windows. Bye, Lily." He chuckled and walked out the door, his rifle slung over his shoulder. *Surely he isn't serious,* I thought. *He can't be.* But did I *really* know what my dad was capable of doing? For a few minutes I pondered whether or not to call Anthony—just in case. *Should I, shouldn't I?* I wondered. Oh, what the hell, better safe than sorry, I decided, so I called. Anthony must have thought my dad was crazy, and maybe he thought I was too, but I felt relieved that I had made the call. When my dad finally arrived home, I asked him why he would say something so stupid, and he said, laughing, "Oh, come on—you know I was just kidding." Ha, ha.

The following month I found out I was pregnant. I believed Anthony was the baby's father, but I wasn't one hundred percent sure. After all, I had had sex with my dad once the month before in exchange for Anthony's dinner invitation. The mere thought of my dad being my baby's father made me feel more nauseated than I already was. I walked into the living room where Dad was sitting on the couch and said, "Dad, I'm pregnant," to which he replied, "I expect you to break up with that asshole Anthony right now!" I'd expected that reaction. What I didn't expect was my dad's insisting that I *not* have an abortion. The next morning as I returned from the bathroom after a bout of morning sickness, Dad waited for me at the breakfast table, a happy smile on his face. He shared his elaborately thought-out, cunning scheme: I would have the baby and we would live happily ever after on the piece of property in Quincy. Dad immediately dragged me out to begin shopping for a trailer that would be placed on the property. Standing inside a beat-up old 1950's Airstream trailer my dad really liked, I felt like I was standing in my very own tin can coffin. Dad excitedly explained that I would live there with the baby, Chrissy, and Gumdrop. (Dad never mentioned what would happen to Connor.) I would raise and sell golden retrievers to generate extra income. My dad would stay in San Jose during the week to work and then come up on weekends. We would pretend to be husband and wife, the proud new parents of our beautiful son or daughter. (I wondered, was the baby really ours?) We would have everyone in Quincy believing that we were one big, happy family, living a fairy tale life.

I was furious. And the more eager Dad became to implement his twisted, elaborate deception, the more furious I got. My options were limited. I had no way of supporting the baby alone, I didn't feel comfortable bringing a baby into the world to raise with someone I'd known barely three months, and I questioned whether or not I was ready to be a mother. Moreover, I was not okay with going along with my dad's plan and giving him that kind of power and control over me and my baby. The thought of being that dependent and trapped, forced to live a lie in the middle of nowhere at my dad's mercy, made me feel sick, and a resounding *"hell no"* echoed loudly throughout my entire being. Any doubt or confusion I'd had vanished in an instant. My decision became crystal clear: I would have an abortion.

My dad was angry with me, but Anthony was very understanding, willing to respect and support any decision I made. I felt relieved when I had the abortion. After the abortion Anthony and I continued to date. I was head-over-heels in love with him.

In June Dad and I went to Lake Shasta. Of course, I begged him to let Anthony go too. But he refused. I was very disappointed and frustrated. However, I kept asking anyway, in the hope that my dad might change his mind. "Dad, why can't Anthony come with us to Shasta? Maybe if you give him a chance, you'll find that you like him. I love him, you know. *Please.*" I could see my pleas were falling on deaf ears, but I had to try.

When my "pleases" didn't work, I tried the "whys." "Dad, why can't Anthony go with us to Shasta?"

"Because at night, the two of you would be all over each other—kissing, fondling, and making out in our tent—and that's not okay with me," Dad explained.

"Okay, okay," I said, so happy, at long last, to get a response from my dad. I felt like I was finally getting somewhere. "Then, how 'bout if I promise not to sleep next to Anthony. You can sleep between the two of us. Then can he come with us?"

"I don't know. I'll have to think about it." There was no more talk about Anthony joining us, so as we packed up and headed out to Shasta, I assumed Anthony wasn't invited.

That's fine, I thought to myself, *I'll spend time with Anthony as soon as I get back.*

A couple of days into our camping trip, my dad turned and asked, "So, what was it again you were willing to do had Anthony come with us?"

"What difference does it make? He didn't," I said, annoyed.

"Yeah, I know, but if he had?" Dad asked, again.

"Well, I had promised to sleep on one side of the tent and have Anthony sleep on the other side, with you in the middle. But it doesn't matter, so whatever," I replied. I felt a little irritated by the sore reminder of what hadn't happened.

"Well, I really don't think you would have done that anyway. I know you would've put Anthony's sleeping bag right next to yours," Dad said.

"No! I wouldn't have done that. I promised. And you know I keep my promises, Dad," I angrily replied. *Such a pointless conversation*, I thought to myself.

"Okay, well, let's get going. We need to get some gas for the boat at the marina," Dad said, and off to Holiday Harbor we went. As I walked up the steep ramp toward the marina store I saw someone who looked very familiar—oh my God—it was Anthony, and he was walking toward me. Without time to process what was going on, I hurried back down the ramp toward my dad. Wait, what was I doing? And what was Anthony doing? Anthony wasn't supposed to be here, and Dad would be very, very angry that he was. Anthony caught up with me at the same time my dad did.

"Lily, I invited Anthony here. I knew how much it meant to you," my dad said.

"Wow! Thanks, Dad. You're the best!" I happily declared. Then I accompanied Anthony to his van and helped him gather his stuff. Dad stayed behind to gas up the boat. Next, we all boarded the boat and traveled to our beautiful, secluded campsite.

We spent the warm summer day on the lake enjoying some boating, water skiing, swimming, and fishing, with great tunes playing and an ice chest full of bottles of beer and Dad's and my favorite wine—TJ Swan Mellow Days and Easy Nights. In the evening we sat around the roaring campfire talking, laughing, drinking, and roasting hot dogs and marshmallows. It was so nice to watch my dad finally make an effort to get to know Anthony, acknowledging and respecting my right to choose a new partner and lover. I was in heaven.

"Well, it's getting late. I think it's time to get some sleep," my dad announced as he gave me a look that warned, *Don't forget your promise.* I gave a slight nod to let him know I remembered.

"Okay, Dad," I replied, and then addressed both men. "Well, let's get the sleeping bags unrolled and ready."

"Why don't you and Anthony go ahead, and I will join you in a minute—I have some dishes to do," Dad said.

"Okay," I said, and then turned to Anthony. "Let's go." In the tent, I was sure to arrange my dad's sleeping bag between Anthony's and mine, keeping my promise. I was so excited that the two of them were getting along so well.

It was a chilly night, so I snuggled inside my warm sleeping bag, waiting patiently for the men to do the same. Anthony and Dad made small talk as they settled in for the night. Eventually it became silent, the kind of lull between conversations that always made me feel uncomfortable. In the stillness of the night, I became aware of the sexual sparks between Anthony and me lighting up the dark. Not even my dad rustling next to me in the tent could smother them. I really wished Anthony and I were alone in the tent to act on our desires, but I knew after our trip we would enjoy plenty of alone time and savor every second.

After a few minutes of awkward silence, my dad initiated a conversation about his and Anthony's favorite baseball team, the New York Yankees. Since both Anthony and Dad had been born and raised in New York, they found they had the same loyalty to the Yankees. I was definitely not a New York Yankees fan. In fact, I didn't even like baseball, but that was okay. As the two men went back and forth discussing boring baseball, I turned my thoughts to something more exciting—fantasizing about Anthony and me— about our naked bodies rubbing, our tongues teasing, and how he could make me explode every time he ... *shit—what the fuck?* My thoughts were shattered by my dad's hand silently penetrating my sleeping bag, his probing fingers traveling into my underwear and fondling me, all the while talking it up with an unaware Anthony about Yankees player statistics.

Okay, I thought, *what do I do? What do I do?* My gut instinct was to let out a loud scream, which would cut this baseball bullshit out, right now, and clue Anthony in on my dad's sickening behavior. I had never despised my dad so much as I did at that moment. But I could say nothing. We were alone in the pitch-black night, on a small island tucked away within a large cove somewhere in the vastness of Lake Shasta, far away from any other living soul. I knew Dad did not like Anthony at all. If I were to call out, how could I be sure that my dad wouldn't pull out his gun and kill Anthony like he had threatened to do before, leaving his decomposing corpse in the middle of the lake? Should I wager Anthony's life on my dad's mental state? Perhaps I would be next—surely Dad wouldn't want to be sloppy and leave an eyewitness behind. Dad was too smart for that. What if I was the weak link in his perfect murder plan because I could no longer be trusted? Maybe I was no longer loyal to my dad and would squeal to the cops if he killed the man I loved. And the only way Dad could keep me quiet was to kill me too. Then Dad would surely get away with murder.

Also, I worried about Anthony finding out the truth about Dad and me. I'd kept Anthony in the dark about my sexual relationship with my dad. How would he react? Would he leave me? Would he hate me forever? Would he do something to my dad? Since the possible fallout for my actions was way beyond my control, and the stakes were far too high, I bit my tongue and silenced my outrage in order to keep my beloved Anthony and our relationship safe. As my dad probed and fondled me in the darkness, I wished his violating hand would wither away and die.

On our drive home the next morning, I blurted out, "I hate you, Dad! How could you put your hand in my sleeping bag and feel me up like that while the man I love lay right next to you? You're sick!"

Dad shrugged his shoulders, smiled, and said, "I'm sorry, Lily, I really am, but I'm only human. I was weak, and I couldn't resist touching you. This is really hard for me, letting you go. I can't stand the thought of you making love to Anthony instead of me. It makes me crazy, okay?"

"Like this isn't hard for me too? But you said you wanted me to date. And you promised that you would help me do that. You promised! Don't you remember?"

"Yes, I do want you to date, and I will help you with that. I promise. But, come on now. Anthony? Anthony is a loser. The guy still lives with his parents. He doesn't have a pot to piss in, and he has absolutely nothing to offer you. You deserve someone far better than him."

"Oh, you mean someone like you, Dad? Well, I don't care what he does or doesn't have! There's really nothing you can say to convince me to leave Anthony or to think any less of him—I love him very much! So please, just help me do this. Support me dating Anthony. And be there for me like a *real* father."

Dad gave me his word he would support my dating Anthony and be a real father to me. However, this promise didn't last long. The following week I came home wearing a beautiful fourteen-karat gold heart pendant which Anthony had given me as a token of his love. Unable to control his jealous rage, Dad walked over to me, yanked the necklace off my neck, and threw it onto the floor. I reached for my neck where my necklace had just been, but Anthony's gift was broken. I turned to my dad. "How could you?" I shouted and stormed off in tears. I began to realize that the more I was with Anthony the less I wanted to be with my dad. And when my dad was acting mean and jealous, I didn't want to be around him at all.

Chapter 8
TEMPORARY BREAK

For the rest of the summer and early fall, Dad did his best to keep Anthony and me apart. Dad constantly increased my workload to keep me busy. To get around this, I brought Anthony along with me while I was working. Soon, my dad laid down the law about work and dating. During work there would be no Anthony, and I was allowed to date Anthony only *one* day per week, period. Needless to say, Anthony and I made the most of our one date a week. He would pick me up early, usually around dawn, and drop me home around midnight.

One morning in October, I left the house at around four o'clock in the morning to go fishing with Anthony. Dad was sick. The day before I'd heard him coughing and sneezing, so I had assumed he had a simple cold or flu. After a relaxing morning of fishing at the lake, Anthony and I had lunch and then went to shoot a few games of pool. Later that day we swung by my house so I could change my clothes. I wanted something a little nicer than my dirty and very smelly fishing clothes to wear to dinner. Once inside my dad called me into the kitchen and told me to sit down. He said, "So, you took off this morning with Anthony and didn't even bother to check if I was feeling better? You didn't care enough to find out if I was dead or alive?" According to him, since I had known he wasn't feeling well, I should have cancelled my date and stayed home to prove my undying love and loyalty.

I rolled my eyes. *How childish,* I thought. "Well, are you okay now?"

"Yes," he coughed. "Not like you'd care."

"Whatever," I said, impatient to get back to my date. We had a dinner to get to.

"Choose! Choose right now, Lily. Anthony or me!" Dad demanded as he slammed his fist down angrily on the kitchen table. Shocked, I stood there staring at him, thinking how sick to death I was of him and his constant attempts to break up Anthony and me, and how cruel he was to break his promise to me. Again.

"Anthony! I choose Anthony!" I said. I ran to my bedroom to grab some necessities and headed for the front door, but Dad stopped me.

"Lily, you realize that once you walk out that door, you will no longer be welcome here. You will lose your family, your home, your job, and even your dog. If I were you, I'd think twice before walking away." Without saying a word, I turned and left, slamming the door behind me. As I ran toward Anthony's car, I burst into tears. I felt devastated to leave my dad, my family, and my life behind, and extremely angry with my dad for making me choose.

"Anthony, I don't know what I'm supposed to do. My dad just kicked me out."

Anthony looked at me, confused. "What? Why would he do that?"

I hesitated. What was I supposed to say? *Oh, yeah, my dad was my lover, and he's so jealous of you he hoped if he made me choose between you and him, I would choose him, and you would finally be out of the picture, for good.*

No, I really couldn't imagine myself ever saying that to Anthony.

Instead, I said, "I don't know why, but suddenly he wanted me to either stop dating you or get out. I love you. So I left."

Anthony said I could move in with him. It was awkward moving into Anthony's parents' home. I had never met Anthony's parents before and had no idea what to expect. Anthony and his parents lived in a small nine hundred square foot, three bedroom, one bath condo in San Jose. Dark-wood paneling, gold-veined mirror tiles, and fresh white paint adorned the walls.

Anthony's parents were both Italians in their fifties who had moved from their hometown of Staten Island, New York, four years before. Anthony's mom Marie, a short woman at four feet ten inches tall, had brown eyes, straight brown hair and a small, serious mouth. She took great pride in running her household. Anthony's dad, Mario, was a tan and trim construction worker who left the house for work by five o'clock each weekday morning. Mario, as well as his son, always wore a gold chain with a fourteen-karat gold Italian horn for good luck.

Lying there that first night wrapped tightly in Anthony's arms felt so good. It was nice to know I didn't have to rush home and deal with my dad anymore; I could relax. And the idea of now being able to spend every day, not just one day a week, with Anthony made me very happy. I tried not to think about all I'd lost, but I was so angry that my dad had taken everything from me, punishing me for choosing Anthony instead of him. Fine, I would show him. I stuffed my sadness and let my anger take over.

The next day I went and talked to Max, a private investigator. Max was Dad's despised rival and biggest competitor. "I don't work for my dad anymore." Max looked surprised, but before he could ask me anything, I said, "Please, don't ask. I can't talk about it. It's personal. Let's just say my dad and I had a big falling out, okay?" He nodded, lit a cigarette, and offered me one. I shook my head and continued. "The thing is I want to work for you, Max."

"Hmm...really?" he said as he gently pulled on his beard. He looked slightly intrigued. I wondered if he was smiling because he liked the idea of hiring me, his rival's daughter. "Well then, Lily, tell me why I should hire you."

I took a deep breath. "Because I know my stuff, I've been doing this for over five years now, I'm a hard worker, I never complain, and people really like me." Max just sat there looking at me, not saying anything at all. "Please, Max, I promise I'll do a great job for you if you'll just give me a chance."

It seemed like forever before he spoke. "Okay, Lily," Max eventually said, exhaling a large puff of smoke. "I'll give you a shot. You're hired."

I smiled and shook his hand. "Thank you, Max. I promise you won't be sorry you hired me." I couldn't wait to go to work the next day. Finally, after all these years, I would be working for someone other than my dad.

Later that day I called my mom and told her the good news. It had been a few months since I'd called her. We'd been talking periodically, and our relationship was friendly but somewhat distant. She was happy to hear I'd moved out of my dad's house and wasn't working for him anymore. I always knew she didn't like my being with my dad, and now that I wasn't, I hoped we could get closer. She said she couldn't wait to meet Anthony. I couldn't wait for her to meet him either.

My first weekend at Anthony's home, I saw how everyone but me had a passion for cooking. The kitchen seemed to be their favorite room in the whole house, and the busiest. On Saturday Marie spent most of the day cooking. She made the most amazing homemade ravioli for dinner and for dessert I discovered cannoli and zeppole. On Sunday the boys did the cooking. Anthony's dad cooked up something called cioppino, a seafood stew made with crab legs, clams, and mussels in a rich tomato sauce, which I had never had before, but after I finished my first mouthwatering bowl, I had to have another. Not to be outdone, I tasted my Anthony's simple yet delectable shrimp scampi, which would quickly become one of my favorite dishes. Anthony's Dad told me, "Mangia, Lily, mangia," as he motioned me to eat, smiled, and topped off my glass of red wine. I ate so much food that day I thought I was going to burst.

The next day Marie asked me, "So, I'm gonna do Tony's laundry, do ya want me to do yours, too?"

"Thanks, Marie, but no, I like doing my own," I said as Anthony and I were running out the door to go bowling and see a movie.

That night when we got home not only were Anthony's clothes all washed and put away, but our room was spotless too. She had changed our sheets, made our bed, neatly rearranged all the items on top of the dresser, opened the window, dusted, and vacuumed. It was like Marie provided maid service for her son when he left the house. She had also separated our stuff, hanging all of my clothes on one side of the closet and Anthony's on the other. She'd put all my underwear, previously mixed with Anthony's, into one separate drawer. It felt weird to think she had been touching my underwear.

"Hey, Anthony, did you see what your mom did?" I said, pointing first to our clothes now separated in the closet, and then to my stuff now in a separate drawer in his dresser.

"Sorry about that, Lil. What can I say? It's just how my ma is," Anthony said.

"That's okay, there could be worse things, right?" We laughed. It seemed a bit odd, but I was grateful that I was allowed to live there, so I didn't say anything to her.

The following week Mom came down from Pocatello and finally got to meet Anthony. She liked him. They instantly bonded and talked for hours about cooking, my least favorite subject. I think Anthony liked my mom far better than he did my dad, and at the time I felt the same. Eileen wasn't there. She was back in Pocatello married to Todd now, but it was nice to see Bart again. He'd gotten so big I hardly recognized him. It was great to finally meet my sweet, pretty little sister, Cindy. I also met Pierre, Mom's fifth husband. He was a small, good-looking Frenchman with a big ego. During our conversations no one ever asked about my dad, so I never talked about him. It was the only time I ever saw Pierre. Soon after our visit he and my mom divorced.

One windy Saturday, nearly a month after I'd moved in, and just after my twenty-second birthday, Anthony and I parked my blue RX-7 at the edge of a lush green cow pasture somewhere on Bass Lake Road in El Dorado Hills. The sun had gone down, but there was still enough light to see the black and white cows grazing nearby. I knew it was time to reveal the truth about my relationship with my dad—time for me to trust Anthony completely with the truth I had hidden from everyone else. I wanted him to understand *why*. *Why* I had left home. *Why* my dad had treated him as he had. *Why* my dad had disowned me. I loved Anthony very much. I wanted a life with Anthony and didn't want him to be in the dark about my dad and me a second longer.

I turned to Anthony and asked him to solemnly swear on his life to never tell another living soul what I was about to tell him. He gave me his word. I told him everything.

"I'll kill him," Anthony said.

"What?" I couldn't believe what I was hearing. "Did you hear a word I just said?" I asked, totally bewildered by his reaction.

"Yeah, I heard you. Your sick perverted father had sex with you, and for that he needs to pay," he replied.

"No! You didn't hear me and you don't understand!" I said, frustrated and unsure if I should have trusted Anthony with my big secret. I had hoped that I could tell Anthony anything and everything like I had my dad. I decided to give it one more try. "Anthony, I was in love with my dad. I wanted to have sex with him. Now our sexual relationship is over. There's no one to punish here. If you can't look at my dad now that you know, how can you look at me? Do you hate me too?" I asked sadly, as I looked directly into his eyes.

"No, of course not," Anthony replied.

"Then, please, just try to understand what I'm saying. It's over with my dad. I chose you. I love you. But he's still my dad, so you have to promise me that you won't lay a hand on him or hurt him in any way. I still care about him," I explained with great pain and desperation in my voice. I meant it from the bottom of my heart. Even though I had left home hating my dad, the time away had allowed me to cool off and realize that deep down I still loved him. After all, he was still my father. I needed to get Anthony to understand, or I'd have to leave him. "I told you so that you could understand. I've never told anyone before. I trusted you. Maybe I shouldn't have," I said with tears rolling down my cheeks.

"Okay, okay, please stop crying. I don't want to see you cry," Anthony pleaded as he held and comforted me. "Thank you for trusting me. I know it must not have been easy for you to open up and tell me. It happened, and it's over now. Lily, I'll keep my promise to you. It'll be hard, but no one, not even your father, will ever know that you have told me. I love you." He paused. "Oh my God, it's all starting to make sense now."

"What? Tell me."

"Remember when your father took me bowling?"

"Yes." I nodded, thinking back to when out of the blue my dad had offered to take Anthony out bowling soon after Anthony and I had gotten back from San Francisco.

"Well, I never told you this before because I didn't want to hurt you. But, your father told me that he knew why I liked you."

"Really? Why?"

"He said I only liked you because you have large breasts and a great body."

I shrugged. "Okay."

"But then he warned me that once you had a kid, your breasts would sag to your waist and you would double in size. Can you believe your father would say that?"

"Yeah, actually I can," I said. The truth was my dad had told me the same exact thing. He told me never to have kids. He said it wasn't worth it because if I did, my naked body would be so ugly and repulsive that no man would ever want me. He said that was why he rarely had sex with Betty. "So, what did you say?"

"I told your father that I liked you because there was something special about you, and I saw it each time I looked into your eyes, like I do right now." He smiled at me and I smiled right back. "Lil, it shocked the hell out of me," Anthony said, shaking his head. "I had never, ever expected to hear *any* father speak that way about his daughter. And you know what else he did?"

"What?"

"When we were in San Francisco, my ma told me that your father came to our home, and he told my parents some bad things about you."

"Bad? Like what?"

"He said that you were a speed addict, constantly drinking and always in trouble, and sexually active with lots of boys."

"What an asshole! Sometimes my dad really pisses me off!"

Anthony nodded. He understood everything now. I lit a cigarette and looked out the half open window at the grazing cows, trying to calm down before driving home.

Later that week at a Pleasure Party, I bought a bottle of cinnamon flavor Emotion Lotion, which the saleslady put in a small brown paper bag. I couldn't wait to try it out on Anthony that night.

As soon as I walked through the front door, Marie asked, "What's in the bag, Lily?"

"Oh, well." I wasn't quite sure how to put it. "It's just a personal item," I said, smiling.

"What? No, I wanna see what's in there, now! Give it to me!" she demanded, trying to take the bag from my hand. I felt confused. She had always been so nice before. I immediately held the bag up out of reach, but this short, spunky little woman who reminded me of a Munchkin kept jumping up, trying to grab it. Finally, she stopped jumping and said, "Fine, I don't need to look in the bag. I already know what's in it!"

"Really," I said, feeling very embarrassed that she somehow did know. "So, what's in here then?"

"Drugs! I know you have drugs in that bag!"

"Drugs? No, sorry, but you're so wrong!"

"I know it's drugs! I know it! And don't tell me it's not!"

"Ma, stop, take it easy!" Anthony said as I ran to Anthony's bedroom and slammed the door. I turned the TV up to drown out the yelling.

A few minutes later, Anthony came in. He turned down the TV. I took out the lotion and showed it to him. He smiled and then said, "Why don't you just show my ma? Show her how silly and wrong she's being to think you have drugs in the bag."

"Look, I really appreciate your mom letting me live here. I really do. But, I should have a right to some privacy, you know? I'm sorry, but it just feels wrong, not to mention embarrassing, to have to show her my Emotion Lotion."

"Well, if that's how you feel, then okay. You don't have to show her anything if you don't want to. I get it. I understand."

"Thanks, I'm glad that you do."

"You know, it doesn't help matters any that your father told my ma you were a drug addict."

"Yeah, I know."

"I understand now why your father was saying all those things about you, but my parents don't. I told them not to believe your father, but they have no reason not to believe him."

"Yeah, and I wouldn't even want to try to explain how my dad was my jealous lover back then."

"No. They would *never* understand that. And, to be quite honest, Lil, I barely do myself."

I nodded. A moment later I asked, "So, if your mom really believed all those horrible things my dad said about me, then why has she been so nice to me?"

"Because I asked her to," Anthony said. "But I guess she just can't do it anymore."

The next day, Marie began giving Anthony a hard time, urging him to see a therapist. She thought there must be something seriously wrong with her son if he wanted to be with me. Marie wanted her son to marry an Italian woman who would cook, clean, and take care of him like she did. As far as she was concerned, I was a drug addict and had nothing to offer her son but trouble, my dad's lies always lingering somewhere in the back of her mind.

Soon after, Marie stopped talking to me. She avoided looking at me and pretended I didn't exist. She resented the close relationship Anthony and I had. Complaining about her rudeness and mean behavior to Anthony only added fuel to the fire. I dreaded coming home and spent most of my time in Anthony's bedroom, away from Marie. Life there was incredibly awkward because of the tension between Marie and me.

Chapter 9
THE TRUTH

After five months of constantly hearing private eye Max, my new boss, smugly gloat over his rival's misfortune with comments like "Gee, Bill. I don't know what happened between you and your daughter, but I'm so glad Lily's working for me now. My clients love her—she's a hard worker and great for business," my dad reluctantly admitted defeat. Dad called and offered to make me an equal partner in his PI business. It was the first time we had spoken since I had left. I agreed to accept Dad's offer only if he would agree to accept Anthony as my boyfriend. Dad agreed, and I believed him. I had to. Deep down, I missed him terribly. I wanted to finally have what I'd thought I never could have—a sex-free relationship with my dad and a boyfriend he accepted.

I gave Max my notice and thanked him for giving me a chance and hiring me. He was sorry to see me leave but didn't seem too surprised. He knew when he hired me that if I worked things out with my dad, I'd quit.

It was so nice to be back working with my dad, and his clients, now "our" clients, were happy to have me back too. Before long Dad and I were talking and laughing and joking around like we always had. And every once in a while, when I would mention Anthony and how well we were getting along, Dad seemed to be okay with it.

In May, almost two months after becoming a partner in Dad's PI business, I went into Anthony's bedroom and told him I couldn't live there anymore. I had tried, but I couldn't take Marie's contempt toward me any longer. I had lived there for seven months, and she had been ignoring me for six. "I miss my family. My dad has a room for rent, and I want to move back home. You're welcome to go with me, but I know how much you struggle with your feelings toward my dad, so I'd totally understand if you don't want to. You can stay here, and we can still date."

"No, I don't want to stay here. I want to be with you," Anthony replied firmly. I smiled because I knew I would be much happier having Anthony with me.

"Do you really think you can live under the same roof with my dad and pretend you know nothing about our past relationship?" I asked, hoping that Anthony could meet this required condition.

"Yes, I know it was something that happened and it's over. You're with me now. I will be fine with it. I love you, Lily, and I want to be with you," Anthony explained. I was so happy that Anthony finally understood. I had missed my family terribly and was tired of Anthony's.

The following week Anthony and I moved into my dad's latest rental home—his third in seven months—a two story, five bedroom house on Sarasota Drive in San Jose. Dad was eager to rent out his last available room for the extra income.

On the first floor were the living room, dining room, kitchen, and my dad's large bedroom, which doubled as our PI office. Since I had no commute to work, life couldn't have been easier, and it was great to have Gumdrop around again too.

On the second floor were four bedrooms occupied by Anthony and me, my sister Chrissy, Evette and Scott, and Evette's little sister Diana.

Evette was a twenty-one-year-old, blonde-haired, blue-eyed bad girl. She had been convicted of robbery and assault and sentenced to one year in Elmwood Correctional Center for Women in Milpitas. She claimed there was no woman in Elmwood who could kick her ass, and I believed her.

Evette's thin, wiry twenty-three-year-old boyfriend Scott was a water quality control technician. Every morning, Scott would get his tall black Tupperware coffee cup, pour his coffee, add a quarter cup of sugar, stir, and attempt to drink his mixture with one trembling hand as he smoked his cigarette with the other. He said he liked the buzz of crank. He also said he and Evette fought a lot, and their fights could get very physical.

Diana was a sweet and attractive sixteen-year-old with long flowing blonde hair who possessed the bluest eyes I had ever seen. She had dropped out of high school and had a boyfriend who was much older than she.

My brother Connor was the only one who didn't have his own bedroom; he had only a closet and a small-sized dresser placed inside the closet in which to store all of his belongings. Without a bed, he slept on the couch. Shortly after Anthony and I moved into Dad's house, Connor left and moved in with Rick. Connor said he loved living at Rick's and having his very own room.

On weekdays, Anthony would leave in the morning to go to work, and I would leave to do my court run. Many evenings and weekends Scott, Evette, Diana, Anthony, and I would sit downstairs watching MTV. Sometimes Chrissy would join us. Dad wasn't home much. He was usually out somewhere with one of the neighborhood boys he hung out with and sometimes took on jobs. Maybe they were out working, or maybe they were at Golfland playing. No one really knew for sure.

———

Later that summer, my roommate Scott and I walked over to Henry Park at the end of our street to play with Gumdrop. I sat on the cement tabletop, dangling my feet off the side while Scott stood next to me. We took turns throwing the green fuzzy tennis ball as far as we possibly could and laughing at how fast Gumdrop retrieved it, dropping the wet ball at our feet and looking up at us eagerly, drool dripping from her mouth, her tail wagging wildly, her stare never wavering from our faces. As I sat there staring back at her, I wondered how many dogs had cool black spots on their pink tongues like she did. *So unique*, I thought. I picked up the ball and threw it as far as I could. Gumdrop was so easily pleased.

"Oh, shit, it's Tommy," Scott said as a tall awkward-looking boy wearing a baseball cap walked toward us. "I haven't seen you in a while. How the fuck have you been, dude?" Scott asked. I had met Tommy, a friend of Dad's, a couple of times before. He was a sad and silently angry thirteen-year-old with crazy girl hair, a strange long face, big protruding ears, and buck teeth. He was known as the "skinny loser."

"Just hangin'," Tommy replied. He turned to me and said, "Lily, I hate to be the one to tell you this, but your dad's fucked up. He's one sick asshole."

Before I could respond, Scott said protectively, "What the fuck are you talking about?"

"Dude, he took me way up into those fucking hills up there," Tommy said angrily, pointing up to the foothills. "You know, way the fuck up there, past Sierra out into the boonies on Mount Keller Road, in the fucking middle of nowhere, and wanted to touch my fucking dick."

"No fucking way. Not my dad," I said, shaking my head. I knew Tommy and Scott had no idea about my past sexual relationship with my dad, but I couldn't believe my dad would do something like that with a boy. I knew my dad didn't like boys; he liked girls, but I had no interest in sharing my personal inside knowledge with them.

"Yeah, no fucking way," Scott agreed as he gently patted Gumdrop's head. "Bill ain't like that."

"Hey man, I'm telling you the truth. That motherfucker offered me fifteen bucks if I would give him a blow job," Tommy said in disgust as he attempted to tuck stray pieces of his wild nappy brown hair back under his cap. "I was so fucked up by what Bill did to me that I tried to kill myself, and now my parents have me in therapy."

Scott and I looked at each other. We didn't know how to take Tommy and his news. On the one hand he sounded so sincere, but on the other hand, his accusations sounded so crazy. "Well, we gotta get back," Scott said.

"Yeah," I agreed. "Come on, Gumdrop, let's go home. Bye, Tommy."

"Later, Tommy," Scott said.

Back home, while Dad was busy in his PI office doing paperwork, Scott shared what Tommy had told us with Evette and Diana out in the living room. Then everyone began speculating about whether or not it was possible that Dad would do such things. I stayed quiet, and when asked what I thought, I just shrugged. Later, Chrissy came out of Dad's office and said Dad wanted to talk to me.

"Hi, Lily," Dad said. He closed the door and sat at his desk. "I hear there are rumors going around about Tommy and me—that I wanted to touch his penis or something."

"Yes, Dad, people are talking," I said, uninterested, because I didn't care about rumors.

"Well, if anyone knows that the rumors aren't true, it's you. You know I'm not gay."

"Okay," I replied. Of course I knew. We'd had our fair share of great sex, and the last time I checked, I was a female, not a male.

"Lily, I want you to do me a favor. I want you to go out there and tell Scott, Evette, and anyone else who accuses me of such a stupid thing, that you don't believe your dad would ever touch Tommy or any other boy."

"Why would it matter what I say or believe?" I asked, reluctant to be part of such a crazy allegation.

"Because people believe you. You're honest and smart. If you say that's how you feel, they'll trust your judgment. You will help put an end to this stupid rumor. So will you do this one small favor for your dear old dad?"

"Sure, if you think it'll help," I said. Dad nodded.

I did what Dad had asked and announced to my roommates that I didn't for one minute believe Tommy's crazy allegations, which I didn't.

When Dad was asked whether or not there was any truth to Tommy's accusations, he laughed it off, saying that something was wrong with Tommy, as he spun his pointer finger in a circle next to his head to indicate Tommy was crazy. "After all, that's why Tommy needs to go to a therapist." And we all laughed, never doubting Dad's innocence.

The next day, I came home to find twelve-year-old Chrissy alone, deep in thought, slowly mopping the kitchen floor. It was unlike her to choose to stay behind to do chores while Dad left to have fun without her. I asked her if she was okay, and she said yeah. But I sensed something was very wrong. I thought back to a few weeks before, when Chrissy got so angry at my dad for taking off and leaving her behind that she punched a hole in the wall. I knew what it felt like to be that angry when Dad had left me behind, back when we were together, so I decided to just come out and ask, "Are you having sex with Dad?"

Startled, she instantly said, "No!"

I wanted to believe her like I had before. "Okay," I said, "just promise me that if you ever need to talk to me about anything that's bothering you, you will." I added, "You know, Dad and I used to have sex, and I'd want better for you, Chrissy." Chrissy stared at me but said nothing. That was something I had never told her before, but for some reason I felt the need to then.

Two weeks later, Chrissy knocked on my bedroom door, ready to talk. In tears, she finally admitted that she was having sex with Dad. She explained that she just couldn't take it anymore. One year before Dad and Chrissy had made an agreement that if she did *everything* he asked of her—sex, cooking, cleaning, etc.—for one year, at the end of that year he would buy her the pony of her choice. Chrissy, suspicious about the dubious proposition, insisted on having the pony promise in writing. "No problem," Dad said, smiling, as he took out a piece of paper and spelled out their agreement. After signing and dating the agreement, Dad handed it over to an elated Chrissy, who immediately hid the document in her bedroom for safekeeping.

For the next year Chrissy did everything asked of her so that she could have a pony of her very own. She patiently counted down the days. Finally, on her twelfth birthday, she woke Dad up and said, "Get up! It's my birthday. Let's go get my pony."

With a quizzical glance, Dad said, "Pony? What are you talking about, Chrissy? I never promised you a pony." Infuriated, Chrissy ran as fast as she could upstairs to her bedroom and took out the promissory letter she had hidden away. She eagerly gave it to Dad to jog his memory. Amused, Dad took the paper and leisurely looked it over. Then a devious smile came over his face and he began to laugh.

"What?" Chrissy questioned angrily.

"Chrissy," he said shaking his head, "this isn't valid. I signed 'Capello' with one 'l', not two." Then he shrugged and walked away, chuckling under his breath. Chrissy just stood there alone, her body shaking, tears streaming down her face.

Devastated, Chrissy finally told me everything. She told me that she and Dad had been having sex regularly for eight years, since before she had even met me. After having sex, he'd buy her things or take her places. She was so happy when I moved in because he'd go to her room only once a week instead of three times a week.

Now Chrissy was crying and unable to meet my eyes. I put my arms around her and said, "God, Chrissy, I'm so sorry. I'm so, so sorry you had to go through all of that."

Chrissy nodded. Then her sadness turned to rage. "I hate Dad! I can't believe he tricked me like that! I just wanted my pony!" I felt Chrissy's anger and frustration as if it were my own. I wondered how my dad could be so cold and heartless. Chrissy was just a child. Suddenly, I had a strong urge to run downstairs and cut off my father's penis with a knife. But instead, I swallowed my rage and gave Chrissy a drag off my cigarette—she'd been smoking for several months—because I felt like she needed it far more than I did. "I had my pony all picked out, too," Chrissy said. "I found him at that stable over by Rick's house, and I had the guy there promise me that he wouldn't sell him because my dad was going to come and buy him for my birthday."

As I listened to Chrissy, I tried to hold myself together as best I could. I was so numb with shock I couldn't even cry. Chrissy looked up at me and asked, "So, now what, Lily?"

I shrugged. "I don't know. I'm going to need a little time to figure all of this out. But for now, can you just act like you normally do, like nothing has changed?" Chrissy nodded. "And Chrissy, whatever you do, please don't tell Dad that you told me." I couldn't even imagine what my dad would do to me, or to Chrissy, if he knew that Chrissy had told me about their sexual relationship.

"I won't," Chrissy said. "I promise."

Chrissy walked out of my room just as Anthony walked in. He closed the door behind him. I sat on the bed in a daze staring out the bedroom window.

"Lil, what's wrong?" Anthony asked. I told Anthony everything Chrissy had said. Anthony was in shock too.

"I can't believe my dad could be *that* cruel, *that* sick," I said as Anthony held me tight. "I was thinking I'd go over to Rick's and tell him everything, but I'm not sure if I should."

"Why not?"

"Well, I know he's my brother, but I don't really know him all that well, and it would feel so awkward talking to him about this."

"Lil, you don't have to do this alone. I think you should go talk to him. What's the worst that could happen?"

I thought about it for a moment. "Yeah, that's true. It's not like things could get any worse than they are now." Or so I thought.

I drove over to Rick's house to share this newfound information with him. Rick and I sat in his living room. After I shared Chrissy's story with him, Rick drew a breath and said, "Me, too."

"What?!" I was shocked. Hands shaking, I lit a cigarette.

Rick added, "I became friends with a male foster kid that had come to live with us when I was a teenager." Rick drew another breath and said, "Him, too."

I shook my head in disbelief. Then, since Rick and I were having a heart-to-heart, I took a deep breath and said, "Me, too." Rick sat silent, speechless—he had never suspected that Dad was having sex with me or Chrissy. He thought Dad had sex with only boys.

I drew another breath and asked, "Connor, too?"

Rick paused. "Hmm, good question. I don't know. I'll have to ask him when he gets home."

"Let's see, Dad had sex with you, me, Chrissy, and a foster kid. Wow, this is a lot to take in, isn't it?" I asked as I put out my cigarette in the small ashtray on the end table between us.

"Yeah," Rick said. He looked at me, his brown eyes serious. "You know, when I was little I used to think all dads had sex with their sons, that it was normal. I thought it was just Dad's special way of showing me that he loved me."

"Yeah, well, I always thought Dad only had sex with me," I said, glancing down at the perfectly stacked magazines on the coffee table. I didn't know which devastated me more, the thought of Dad having sex with Chrissy or the thought of Dad having sex with Rick. For some reason, I had no idea how to even begin to process the thought of Dad having sex with a boy. I found myself drowning in a Dad-made sea of lies and deceit.

But I knew we needed to do something so that Dad would stop abusing Chrissy. I stared at the dark windows. "So, now what do we do?"

Rick pondered. "The million dollar question. One thing's for sure, Dad definitely needs help."

"I agree. So, how do we get him help?" I asked.

"I have no idea," Rick replied. "We need to talk to someone."

"I know a good attorney, let's talk to him."

Later that evening, Rick told Connor everything and asked if Dad had had sex with him too. Connor said no. Dad had asked Connor to have sex several times, but each time Connor refused.

It finally made sense why Dad had treated Connor so badly. I'd had absolutely no idea that Connor was such an extraordinarily courageous child, standing strong by his convictions, completely alone, no matter the cost.

The next day Rick and I talked with an attorney who recommended that we speak with Art, the director at Parents United, a comprehensive program that offered individual and family therapy where there was molestation by a family member.

Rick and I met with Art, a very large man, in his small and cluttered San Jose office. At first glance Art was intimidating, but I couldn't get out of my mind how he looked just like the kind and gentle TV character Grizzly Adams, except clean-shaven. Dressed in jeans and a red checkered flannel shirt, he seemed down to earth and immediately put us at ease.

"We're here because we want to get our dad some help," Rick said.

"That's right," I said anxiously, as Rick and I both paced around the office, too restless to sit.

"Well, of course you do," Art said in a soft-spoken voice. "When sexual abuse occurs, the entire family needs treatment. Please, sit, and let me explain how Parents United can help you, your family, and your dad." Rick and I looked at each other, shrugged, and sat. Art told us about Parents United's various support groups, therapies, resources, and programs designed to help both victims and offenders. After we told him about the situation, he said, "Our ultimate goal is to reunite both of you, Connor, and Chrissy back with your father." Rick and I looked at each other and smiled. We liked the thought of that.

"And I want to tell you that the program your dad would be in, the Parents United Adult Incest Offender Treatment Program, works. I should know. I was a molester," Art confessed. Rick and I didn't know what to say. We were shocked that this gentle, compassionate man was a molester like our dad. Art explained how therapy had changed his life. He said that by going through the program, he was able to break the cycle of abuse and eventually mend his relationship with his daughter, whom he'd molested. Art continued, "Not only did it work for me, but Parents United has a 98% success rate in treating molesters nationwide."

"Wow, 98%? What do you think, Rick?" I asked.

"I'd say those are pretty good odds. I think Parents United can help our dad," Rick replied.

"The first step is to report your dad to the police. Most offenders will not stop until there is an intervention, and your dad cannot be allowed to continue to molest Chrissy," Art said.

"*Call the cops*? I don't know if I like that idea," I said. Going behind my dad's back and turning him in to the cops felt scary and wrong.

"No, we don't want our dad to go to jail. We just want to get him some help," Rick said.

"I understand your concerns, but he must be reported before we can help him. I can't guarantee that your dad will not do some prison time, but between you and me, he most likely won't, and if he does, it will be minimal if he agrees to get help through a program like ours. I can't stress enough that without help he *will* continue to molest Chrissy. So, are you ready to take the first step? Are you ready to stop the incest once and for all, and get your dad the help he needs?" Art looked from Rick to me, his gaze serious.

"Yeah, okay," Rick and I both said, although we were nervous about what might happen.

"Okay, then, I'll make a call to Sergeant Steele, a friend of mine over at the San Jose Police Department." Art reached for the black phone on his messy desk. "I'll tell him you're on your way."

Later that afternoon, Rick, Chrissy, and I spoke with Sergeant Ron Steele. He was a big man who treated us with a lot of kindness and patience when taking our statements.

Rick informed Sergeant Steele that from the ages of eight to thirteen, Dad had fondled Rick's penis, put Vaseline on Rick's thighs, and rubbed his own penis between Rick's thighs until Dad ejaculated.

In the report, Chrissy also described sex with Dad. He would take off his clothing, take off hers, fondle and kiss her breasts and vaginal area, spread Vaseline on her inner thighs, and rub his penis up and down her legs, coming either on her or on a towel. This had occurred one to three times per week since she was four years old. Chrissy also stated that if she wanted a pair of shoes or clothing, she would first have to go to the bedroom with her dad and allow him to fondle her and use Vaseline to come, and then he would buy her the item she wanted.

To the police I gave a detailed statement of having sexual intercourse at various locations (cabin in Tahoe, my dad's office, the woods) with my dad from the ages of sixteen to twenty-one. Sometimes Dad would put Vaseline on my thighs and rub his penis between my legs while touching and kissing me until we both came. I stated that I had "fallen in love" with my father, and I had been led to believe that our secret fairy-tale romance was purely monogamous after my stepmother Betty had passed away.

Sergeant Steele said Dad would be arrested the following day. Rick, Chrissy, and I decided it would be best if we didn't tell Dad. We had no idea what Dad would do if he knew. So the plan was to go home and act normal, as difficult as that would be.

Chapter 10
THE INVESTIGATIONS

On September 8, 1983, Sergeant Ron Steele and his partner walked into the video store where my dad had recently started working part-time and arrested him for suspicion of child molestation. Sergeant Steele handcuffed my dad, informed him of his rights, and escorted him to the San Jose Police Department for questioning.

Meanwhile, Chrissy, Anthony, and I, without telling our roommates Evette, Scott, and Diana, made a mad dash through the house and grabbed our things. I took Dad's old black photo album, the one with pictures of me when I was little. As I was running out the front door, I grabbed my favorite Tahoe photo from the mantel. I went around the side of the house and took my dog Gumdrop too. We threw our stuff into Anthony's van and drove the two miles to Rick's house. I put the Tahoe photo on Rick's mantel next to his young daughter's photo. For some reason I wanted the photo near me.

That day, as we were moving in, Rick's wife was moving out. Once she had heard about our dad's molestations, she didn't want her daughter anywhere near our sick father ever again. But Rick refused to go along with this. He loved his dad very much and would not agree to keep his daughter from her grandfather. That was not okay with Rick's wife, so she took her daughter and left like my mom had when she found out Carlos had been molesting me. I didn't realize until much later how incredibly brave my mom was to walk away from everything she had built with Carlos and start again, motivated by her desire to protect me from being molested as she had been. I'd never been prouder of my mom than at that moment, and I had to wonder if one day Rick's daughter would feel the same way about her mom, too.

Rick was completely devastated. He loved his wife and daughter more than life itself, and now they were gone.

The following week Rick announced that he had become a born-again Christian. It seemed like he always had a Bible in his hand and was always citing verses. I was glad Rick found comfort in religion, but I found his constant preaching annoying, as did everyone else.

After my dad was arrested, routine police investigations began. Interviews with Dad's siblings revealed molestations between siblings and very possibly included sexual abuse between mother and children and stepfather and children.

Dad explained during his interview that incest was a common activity in the home in which he was raised. He recalled that when he was twelve, his older brother, who Dad said was "one horny bugger," would spread Dad's thighs with Vaseline and thrust his penis in and out between his thighs until his older brother ejaculated. Dad didn't recall being afraid of his older brother, just confused. Now it was clear where my dad had learned this sexual act, the same one he felt compelled to repeat with each of us. His older brother had also molested his eldest sister, while his stepfather had had an incestuous relationship with Dad's other sister from the ages of twelve to fifteen.

Dad exhibited signs of denial and confusion when he stated that he did not believe in premarital sex. When asked how he could justify allowing teenagers to have live-in relationships in his home, Dad stated that he "had no control over that." When asked how he could justify having sex with his daughters he stated that he "didn't have sex with Chrissy and had no intention of marrying Lily."

Next, the police interviewed former next-door neighbor Ruth. She said Betty and Bill did not sleep together when they first married; instead, Bill slept in Rick's room with Rick, then eight years old. Ruth added that Bill had spent far more time with neighborhood boys than with Betty. He always had little boys around him, and they were usually poor and from broken homes. Ruth and Betty both suspected Bill of having sex with these boys but were never able to gather any solid proof, although they noticed that Bill always kept an open bottle of Vaseline in his car.

After interviewing Ruth, Sergeant Steele stopped by Rick's house and asked Rick and me if there were any other children that Dad spent time with—children that he might have had an opportunity to molest too. Even though I was aware that my dad was often in the company of slender young boys (typically thirteen years of age or younger), I'd never thought he was having sex with any of them. I'd never imagined my dad to be anything other than a heterosexual man, so I had no reason to think that these innocent boys with baby faces were any more than friends and companions, company for my dad while he worked. But now I was worried.

Rick and I provided the sergeant with a list of the names of the boys we knew Dad hung around with.

I walked Sergeant Steele out, and we found Anthony standing in the driveway smoking a cigarette while talking to Connor. "You know, Anthony," Sergeant Steele said, "if I were you, I'd run as far and as fast as I possibly could to get away from Lily and her dysfunctional family. In all my years of investigating cases, this is by far the worst I've ever seen." Anthony nodded slightly, put his cigarette out, and slowly walked back into the house. I stared at the sergeant with angry eyes. How dare he say something like that to my boyfriend.

"Well, Connor, I hope you've said your goodbyes to your father," Sergeant Steele said.

"Why? What do you mean?" Connor asked, scared to death by this passing comment. Connor had already lost his mom; he didn't want to lose his dad too.

"There's nothing worse you can be in prison than a child molester," the sergeant said. "And once it's known what your father has done, he'll probably be beaten and raped and eventually killed by the other inmates." Connor and I stood there stunned and watched Sergeant Steele walk to his car and pull away.

"Don't worry, Connor," I said. "Dad's not going to prison." At that point none of us really thought there was much chance of that happening. Instead, we assumed Dad would be put on probation and go through the Parents United Adult Incest Offender Treatment Program, getting the help he so desperately needed, as Rick and I had discussed with Art. We thought everything was going to be okay.

Once Dad made bail, he frantically called each boy he had spent time with. One mother told Sergeant Steele that Bill continued to phone even after she had told him that her son was not home and had demanded that he stop calling. But Dad kept calling every hour until he finally reached her son. While I don't know what my dad told each boy, I do know that each boy Dad had contacted told Sergeant Steele exactly the same thing: Bill had never touched him inappropriately, ever.

There was only one boy who did not get the call from Dad before the police came to interview him at his home—Tommy, the boy who two months before had told me Dad had offered him money in exchange for a blow job.

Tommy had met Dad in the spring of 1982 when he got a job as a paperboy for the San Jose Mercury News. Dad had the newspapers at his home, and each morning Tommy went to Dad's house to prepare his newspapers for home delivery.

By the summer of '82, Dad was taking Tommy on outings such as bowling, miniature golfing, and playing arcade games. He also brought Tommy to work and taught Tommy how to drive.

In his statement to Sergeant Steele, Tommy gave the details of his relationship with my dad. In the police report, Tommy stated that in the winter of 1982, he went with Bill to Lake Tahoe. They made a stop over in the Placerville area to sleep in Bill's van. Bill supplied twelve-year-old Tommy with alcohol. Bill attempted to massage Tommy's penis through his pants, and then tried to insert his hand down Tommy's pants. Tommy ran from the van, went to a nearby restaurant, and phoned home for bus fare, afraid to ride home with Bill.

Tommy must have really missed my dad and his attention, because after that night Tommy reported being in Dad's van several more times where my dad again attempted to have sexual contact with him. On several occasions Dad tried to fondle Tommy's penis and offered Tommy fifteen dollars to give him a "head job." Tommy never stated in the police report if he had accepted any of my dad's offers.

When I found out that Tommy had been telling me the truth in the park that day, I cried. I felt so bad for him and all he had been through. I felt terrible for not believing him and for all of us laughing at him.

Meanwhile, my dad was given a battery of tests, all of which were later submitted to the court. The first test was the Minnesota Multiphasic Personality Inventory, a test which required him to indicate true or false to a series of questions about his beliefs and attitudes. The test results showed that my dad had adequate control of his impulses, tended to deny his problems, and had no insight into his behavior. Although he may have had chronic anger that went unexpressed, he controlled his anger and did not express anti-social behavior. The doctor felt that if Dad's defense system were to be broken down, he could possibly have a full psychotic break. His defense system kept him stable.

A week and a half later, another doctor administered the Thematic Apperception Test (TAT). This test required my dad to respond quickly to pictures that tended to evoke strong responses. The test showed a very different picture of my dad than did the Minnesota Multiphasic Personality Inventory test. The TAT test showed clear signs of sexual problems. The test results indicated that he preferred close relationships with minors (boys and girls) rather than with mature women. He possessed angry feelings about my seeking the affections of Anthony, which he viewed as my being unfaithful to him. He perceived that his sexual infidelity was not a problem unless he got caught. He had feelings of anger toward those who disrupted his relationships, and had no sense of consciousness as to why the disruptions might be appropriate. Lastly, implicit in his responses were considerable unresolved feelings he had toward women his own age, which resulted in his not seeing them as attractive and his needing to withhold affection from them.

This doctor noted that under the clear structure of an interview, Dad was able to put his best foot forward as long as he was functioning on a superficial level in describing events. In order to stay superficial, he would avoid the discussion of details or what he thought, maintaining considerable emotional distance from the task and then periodically going "blank," claiming to not know what he was thinking, or giving many tangential answers. Because of this, the doctor felt that insight therapy like that used in the Parents United programs would be of no value to my dad.

The last test Dad had evaluated his sexual preferences. He was hooked up to a penile plethysmograph, a device which measures any slight increase in the size of the penis due to increased blood flow as a result of sexual arousal. While hooked up to the device, Dad listened to tape recordings of both illegal and socially acceptable sexual scenarios. The plethysmograph then measured the degree of sexual arousal experienced in response to these scenes.

When Dad listened to tapes of socially acceptable sexual scenarios, he measured a very low level of arousal. The highest arousal level was in response to scenarios of fondling and sex play with his daughter Chrissy. The next highest arousal level was in response to a sexual fondling scene of Rick that occurred some fifteen years before when Rick was thirteen. Dad showed no arousal in response to sexual scenes with me.

The police investigations and tests were revealing a father I didn't want to know, a monster who scared me. The man I loved, the man I trusted, the man I thought I knew completely, had been living a double life.

Chapter 11
NERVOUS BREAKDOWN

Late one afternoon almost two months after Dad had been arrested, I sat in Rick's house and kicked my bare feet up on the coffee table. I was alone, glad that Rick wasn't there to complain, "Lily, could you please get your feet off my table?" I tried to relax, but I couldn't stop thinking about Chrissy. Ever since we'd moved to Rick's house, Chrissy had been a handful. She had tried running away and started cutting classes at the alternative school we had placed her in. Rick and I were terrified when she had taken an overdose of pills, both of us having flashbacks of Betty's suicide. At the hospital, Chrissy had her stomach pumped and made it through okay, this time. But we didn't want there to be a next time. Rick and I had Chrissy start counseling with a Parents United therapist, but she hated going. The only person she really wanted to talk to was her dad.

Suddenly the phone rang, making me nearly jump out of my seat. It was Art. "Lily, now that a boy from outside your family has come forward and given his statement detailing your dad's molestation, your dad will no longer be eligible for our Parents United Adult Incest Offender Treatment Program," Art said.

"No longer eligible? What are you talking about, Art?" I asked, confused.

He sighed softly and continued. "Unfortunately, when an offender goes outside his family to seek and molest a child, he is beyond our help. I was not given any indication when we met that your dad had molested outside the family. I'm sorry."

"Wait. What? I thought you said your program had a 98% success rate," I asked him, still confused. When Rick and I had met with Art, we didn't know Dad had molested outside the family either, and I couldn't understand why it mattered.

"At Parents United we deal only with incest offenders or non-predatory, non-pedophilic molesters. Your dad, on the other hand, is what is known as a predatory pedophile. Sadly, more than 50% of convicted predatory pedophiles will be rearrested for a new offense, and they are least likely to benefit from therapeutic intervention," Art explained.

"I still don't understand why you can't help my dad though. I mean, molester or pedophile, aren't all sex offenders basically the same?" I asked.

"No, they're not. But that's a very common misconception. The vast majority of sex offenders, something like 95%, are incest offenders, molesting children in their families. They're much more likely to benefit from therapy programs like those we offer here at Parent's United because deep down they tend to feel very bad about what they've done and want to make things right," Art explained patiently. "But like I've said, your dad's very different. He's a predatory pedophile."

"So? Why does that matter? They all molest kids, don't they?"

"Yes, they all molest kids, but for very different reasons. Did you ever notice how your dad likes to hang around with kids, but not so much with adults?"

"Yeah, so?"

"That's because unlike an incest offender, a predatory pedophile like your dad is sexually attracted to children, whom he'll court or groom for the sole purpose of victimization. And in your dad's case, he feels no remorse."

"Why do you say that?"

"Well, Lily, I hate to be the one to tell you this, but according to the results of the tests your dad took, as well as interviews done with him, he's also what's called a sociopath."

"A sociopath? What does that mean?"

"It means that your dad has no conscience, no sense of guilt or remorse for anything that he does, and will most likely molest again if given the chance. Sadly, our program would make no difference to someone like your dad."

"So what happens to my dad now?"

"Well it's up to the courts to decide, but since your dad wasn't accepted into our program, he'll probably do some prison time. Again, I'm so sorry, Lily, that we're unable to help your dad, but Chrissy's still welcome to continue her free weekly counseling sessions with us. All the best to you and your family during these trying times."

I hung up the phone, Art's words still ringing in my ears. Was this really who my dad was? I cringed in horror when I pictured my dad, a remorseless sociopath, a sexual predator, molesting Tommy in his van, thinking he'd never get caught. How could he do such horrible things? And if I were to believe Art, then Dad would probably never be able to change that predatory part of himself. *Well, isn't that just great,* I thought. *My dad's so broken, he can't even be fixed.* I fell to the floor and sobbed.

That night, I told Rick what Art had said. "What?" Rick yelled. "We didn't do this to send Dad to prison! We did it to get him some help! Art said Dad would get help if we turned him in. So, where's that help?"

"Hey, I wanted Dad to get help too. But like Art said, everything's different now that Tommy came forward about Dad molesting him, and there are probably lots of others, too. Oh my God, Rick,

Dad's not just a child molester. He's a..." I stopped. It felt strange saying it out loud. "A predatory...pedophile. Oh, and a sociopath, too," I said.

"So?" Rick said.

"So, according to Art, someone like our dad really can't be helped," I said teary-eyed.

"Oh, Lily! I don't believe any of that crap about Dad not being able to be helped. And I don't understand why you do," Rick said.

"I don't think it's crap," I said. "I think it's true." Whether or not Dad had molested little boys outside of our family made no difference to Rick, but it made a huge difference to me. Thanks to Art, I now realized that our dad's problem went far beyond incest, and that scared me. Rick didn't want our dad to go to prison, but now I did.

"Well, there's only one thing that really matters anyway and that's forgiveness," Rick said. I rolled my eyes. Ever since Rick had become a born-again Christian, he sounded more like a preacher than a big brother.

"You know, Jesus died for your sins, and mine, and Dad's too. So, if Jesus can forgive Dad for his sins, then I can forgive Dad too. In fact, I have. And the courts should forgive him too. Tomorrow I'm going to explain that to the judge and demand all charges against Dad be dropped immediately." I said nothing as Rick looked through his Bible, underlining the best passages to read in court.

The next day, when Rick got home from Dad's court appearance, he was infuriated that he'd had no authority to stop the case from proceeding, for it was now in the hands of the state. Rick's objections had made no difference whatsoever.

"Oh, and by the way, Dad pled guilty, so there'll be no trial. He'll be sentenced at some later date," Rick explained angrily. I nodded, glad to hear I didn't have to take the stand to testify against my dad. "Dad didn't want to put us through a trial," Rick smiled. "That's how much he cares about us."

I looked at him. "You really think that's why Dad pled guilty, Rick? Because he cares about us?"

"Yes. Why else would Dad do that?"

"Oh, I don't know. Maybe because he figured the judge would go easier on him, and he'd serve less time that way?" Rick glared at me, then turned and walked away, his Bible clutched tightly in his hand. I turned on the TV and tried not to think about Rick or Dad.

The week after Dad's court hearing, while Dad was out on bail, Rick openly ignored the court order stating Chrissy was to have no contact with Dad and dropped Chrissy off at Dad's house when Dad was home. When I found out, I was so angry I couldn't see straight. I hadn't gone through all that I had just to let Dad molest Chrissy again. I confronted Rick. He said Chrissy's seeing Dad again would be the best thing for her. Chrissy believed Dad wouldn't molest her anymore and wanted to be with him.

Even though Connor lived at Rick's, I rarely saw or spoke to him. But one day he told me, "Of course you don't care, Lily. Your mother's still alive. My mom's dead, and my dad is all I have left. If he doesn't make it out of prison alive, I'll *never* forgive you." His eyes filled with tears. I had nothing to say. The truth was if anything did happen to Dad while he was in prison, I didn't think I could forgive myself either. *Shit. How could everything go so horribly wrong?* I wondered.

I didn't dare go to work after I'd turned my dad in. Dad was out on bail, working. It seemed like business as usual for him, but not for me. I often sat home alone worried and slightly depressed. I wasn't even brave enough to go and apply at Dad's competitors because of my fear of running into my dad.

One Friday afternoon in early December, I was home alone. Rick and Anthony had gone to work. Chrissy was at school, I hoped. I felt hungry, so I went to the kitchen and got a slice of Wonder bread, spread on a thick layer of peanut butter, topped it off with a thin layer of strawberry jam, and grabbed a handful of potato chips. As I poured myself a tall glass of milk to go with my sandwich, I was startled by a loud knock at the door, and then another. *Probably some pushy salesperson*, I thought. I stood silently, waiting for him or her to leave. I was hungry and wanted to enjoy my lunch in peace.

"Open up this fucking door right now, you little bitch," Evette angrily screamed as she pounded on the door. "I won't let you fuck over my buddy Bill! I won't let you send Bill to prison! Your ass is mine, bitch!"

No fucking way am I answering that door, I thought. Suddenly in survival mode, I dropped to the ground and lay motionless and silent on the floor, out of view of any window. My heart raced and my body trembled in fear. Evette terrified me. I was not a fighter. I had never learned how. The only thing I knew how to do was cower in a corner like I had done when my mom hit me. *If Evette can kick the ass of a rough and tough Elmwood inmate, what chance could I possibly have?* I wondered.

"What sort of stupid bitch sends her own father to prison? You're so fucked up! Open up this fucking door right now, bitch," Evette screamed at the top of her lungs.

I closed my eyes and prayed I would not see Evette's face or fist today.

"I know you're in there, you stupid bitch. I can hear you, and you can't hide! You better drop these fucking charges against Bill, right now," Evette screamed as she repeatedly banged on the door. "Get out here, Lily. Why you hidin', you chickenshit?" Suddenly I was thirteen, and my mom was egging me on to hit her like she hit me. When I refused, she laughed in my face, calling me a chickenshit. She never let me forget that she was the better and stronger fighter. And I knew she was right. I was not a fighter even though many times I wished that I were, like right now.

Yes, I am chickenshit. I admit it, I told myself. Then, the pounding and screaming stopped. I wondered where Evette had gone. Would she find an open window or unlocked back door? Would she smash a window and climb in? I was too terrified to move or make a sound. I lay motionless another twenty minutes before I felt it was safe enough to move. Like a soldier in war, I crawled to the front window to see whether she'd really gone. I peeked out, being careful not to move the drapes. There was no sign of Evette or her car. I could breathe a little easier, for now.

The next day Les came over for a visit. It was so nice to see Les again. I hadn't seen him for a few months. I thought it would be so much fun if we could go shopping and do some people watching at the mall for old times' sake, but I quickly learned this was not a social call. "Well, Lily, I never told you this before," Les said solemnly, "but when I was a kid, my grandfather molested me and my little brother."

"Really? Wow, I had no idea. Les, I'm so sorry," I said. I thought since we had this experience in common, Les would understand what I was going through, and he would be there for me and support me. We would become even closer friends. And a real friend was exactly what I needed.

"Yeah, well, the thing is we dealt with it as a family. Why didn't you?" Les asked.

"I'm happy you could deal with your grandfather molesting you and your brother as a family, but with my dad it's not the same. Parents United said that once my dad stepped outside the family to molest, he became a predator, and the odds that he will ever change are slim to none. Your grandfather wasn't a predator. You're so lucky," I said as I recalled my last conversation with Art.

"Well, I think you're wrong about your dad and wrong to go to the cops. If you put your dad in prison, I never want to speak to you again," Les said disappointedly as he walked out the door. I felt crushed that my supposed friend did not understand and stand by me, but instead abandoned me. It was the last time I ever saw Les.

The next day a letter came for me from Dad's attorney. *What could Dad or his attorney possibly have to say to me?* I wondered. Part of me was too afraid to open the letter, scared of what it might say. Hands shaking, I slowly tore open the envelope. I read that our partnership had been terminated; therefore, all "our" clients reverted back to my dad and were now legally "his" clients. If I contacted or offered my legal services to any clients in an attempt to lure business away from my dad, I would be sued. The truth was I had spoken to a couple of clients, not in the hope of drumming up business for myself, but because over the years they had become my friends, and in all the chaos I found I really needed someone to talk to. After reading the letter, I cut off the few client friendships I had made. I didn't want any lawsuits from my dad.

Unemployed and needing to earn an income, I began the job hunt. I felt I had enough background and knowledge of the legal world from my PI experience to land a good job. As I began applying for various legal office positions, I found interviewers often pretended to like me and my experience and then not hire me. I didn't have any references. Obviously I couldn't ask for any from my dad, and I felt too ashamed to ask Max after having quit my job. I was growing frustrated and beginning to doubt my ability to find work.

Finally I found an entry-level legal secretary position. Linda, the interviewer, told me I could expect a call Monday to let me know their decision. I had a good feeling about this one. All the other companies I had interviewed with the previous week had rejected me, but I was sure this one would be different. They liked me; I was sure they liked me. That Monday I sat staring at the phone, hopeful Linda would call me any second to tell me the good news. I was actually overqualified, but that was okay. I really wanted the job, a job I had gotten all by myself, without ties to my dad. I looked at the clock. It was two o'clock, and then three. Linda must be extremely busy, but I knew she would call; she had promised me that she would. It was now three forty-five and Linda went home at four. I was convinced she had been too busy to call me, so I would call her. With shaky hands I picked up the receiver and dialed Linda's number. I couldn't wait to hear the good news straight from Linda, and I wouldn't mind her apologies for not calling me herself sooner to give me the good news.

"I'm sorry, Lily, but we decided to hire another candidate who had more experience," Linda said. As soon as I hung up the phone, I realized what she had said, and all hopes of something going right for once were gone. I felt certain that I'd done my very best, confident that I'd made a great impression, and so sure I would be hired. But I had been rejected, again. I felt like such a failure. Maybe I just didn't have what it took to work out in the real world. I sat feeling miserable.

I picked up the photo of my dad when he was my lover and my best friend, kneeling down in the Tahoe snow next to our Gumdrop, and looked at it while thinking how happy I was then.

Although I thought he should go, I was devastated at the thought of my dad in prison. I believed my dad had loved me and wanted me. I had loved him and wanted him. Once our love affair had ended, and I had Anthony, my dad could be very cruel. But I had come to understand. Had my dad found another lover before me, I knew I could have been just as cruel, maybe even more so—my intense jealousy and rage probably would have gotten the better of me. But I'd wanted my dad to move on and be happy like I was. Then, with our affair left in the past where it belonged, I would finally have a normal dad.

But I could never have a normal dad. He was a predator and a pedophile—most of his lovers were little boys. I had thought I understood my dad completely. The realization that I actually hadn't known my dad at all and that I had believed only what he had wanted me to believe infuriated and depressed me to no end.

There is a significant impact on children when a parent is

incarcerated, and for some the price they pay is the greatest penalty of all. Sadly, almost 100% of children who report molestation by a relative answer "no" when asked if they would report the incident if they were molested again. Feeling responsible for the abuse, guilty about reporting the abuse, and guilty for the consequences to the perpetrator are all devastating to a child. In addition, the fear of possible consequences from the family and subsequent retaliatory actions from the perpetrator is why child molestation, like rape, is one of the most underreported crimes: only 1-10% are ever disclosed.

I almost cried out for my dad like I had so many times before but suddenly remembered how this time my dad wasn't going to come rushing through the door to embrace me and make all my pain go away, saving me from myself. That would never happen again because the one person I could always count on to make it all better, I had helped send to prison. Oh, my God! What had I done?

I sobbed. Life seemed far too scary without my dad right there next to me. I hated my dad for all the terrible things he had done, but I hated myself too. I hated myself for missing him so much—his touch, his smell, his voice, his smile. I wanted to take that damn picture of Dad off the mantel, smash it against the wall, and watch the glass shatter into a million jagged little pieces. I wanted to tear the picture to shreds. But for some reason, I couldn't. Instead, I lay curled up on the floor shaking beside the photo, my stomach churning, my head pounding, and my whole body exploding with unbearable pain. Even though I hated my dad, I didn't know how to live without him. I hadn't known how when I was seven, and I sure as hell didn't know how now. And at that moment, I didn't want to.

Lying there, on the brink of suicide, I finally understood why my mom, Betty, and Chrissy had all wanted to commit suicide. It wasn't because they were necessarily weak people, as I had previously thought; it was because they simply wanted the unbearable pain to stop.

I was reaching for the bottle of Valium, ready to commit suicide and end the pain once and for all when suddenly I began to hear a faint whisper inside my head. I heard it again, then again, growing louder and louder. "Wait! Wait!" the voice cried. "What if there's another way? What if there's another choice?" Of course Path A was suicide, a choice that would always be available to me, but what about another possibility, a Path B?

Suddenly, Art flashed across my mind. He was sitting behind his desk at Parents United, telling Rick and me about the pain of incest and how therapy had helped him break the cycle of abuse and changed his life. I had never heard anyone talk so highly of therapy before. I found the idea of speaking to a therapist—a stranger— scary, yet for the sake of choice I would try. But if for some reason it didn't work—if it did nothing to address the pain or added to my suffering in any way, or if I didn't like the therapist or the therapy and felt I was wasting my time—well, then I would take comfort in knowing that Path A could still be my choice. I slowly put the bottle of Valium down and reached for the phone.

I called Art and asked if he could recommend a good therapist. "Yes, absolutely. Sharyn Higdon Jones. She's a Licensed Marriage, Family, and Child Counselor (LMFCC) who specializes in the treatment of sexual abuse victims. Her office is downtown off The Alameda. I've worked with her in the past, so I know firsthand that she's one of the finest therapists around. You'll be in good hands with Sharyn, Lily," Art said.

I thanked him, hung up, and called Sharyn. She was on vacation until after the new year. Her first appointment was in two weeks at 10 a.m.. I said, "Okay, I'll be there."

Later that day, I sat drinking a Budweiser and smoking a cigarette, thinking about the one person still standing next to me, the one person I might trust enough to ask for help—the person who hadn't run from me even though Sergeant Steele had advised him to. I cried out, "Anthony!" the moment I saw him walking up Rick's driveway from work that night. "I need to talk to you, now! Please!" He nodded and I grabbed his hand, led him down the hallway to our bedroom, and closed the door.

"I can't live here anymore. I just can't," I said, then collapsed into Anthony's arms, sobbing, just like I used to with Dad. "I'm dying here. My dad always knew how to help me when I felt this way, but he's not here now. And I just can't do this all by myself. Living here is making me crazy. I feel like a sitting duck, just waiting for something bad to happen."

"What do you mean, Lily?" Anthony asked.

"I mean when you're at work all day, I sit here alone and scared. I jump every time I hear a loud noise, wondering if Evette or one of her thugs has come back to hurt me. When the phone rings I'm afraid to answer it, afraid to hear that Chrissy attempted suicide again, but this time successfully. When the mail comes, I'm afraid I might find another letter addressed to me from my dad's attorney. I just don't feel safe here, Anthony. Also, I'm tired of hearing Rick's constant preaching, and of course I hate that he allows Chrissy to see Dad. The thought of Dad being with Chrissy makes my stomach turn, but Rick doesn't care how I feel about it. He ignores me, and I'm tired of it. I need to get out of here, now. But I have no place to go. Can you find a place where we can go and disappear? And fast. Please, before I die here."

"Okay, I understand. I will do my best to get us out of here as soon as possible," Anthony said. He held me tight and tried to comfort me. I hoped Anthony could find us somewhere else to live. I felt like my life depended on it.

The following morning at work Anthony explained the situation to his boss. His boss said Anthony and I could move in with him immediately, and Gumdrop could come too.

Anthony called me to let me know we had a place to stay. He would pick me up in an hour. It would be easier to leave now when no one was home. No questions. No explanations. We'd just go and disappear. No one would know where I had gone. I liked that idea. I quickly gathered our stuff.

There was one last thing I had to do before I could leave Rick's house. I had to call Chrissy's probation officer. Chrissy was assigned a probation officer soon after Dad had been arrested. The probation officer was Chrissy's child advocate, there to advise, assist, and protect her, and to decide the best place for her live. "I'm sorry, but I just can't do this anymore," I explained to the probation officer. "I'm going crazy living here. It's all just too much, and I've got to get out of here. I'm sorry I can't be Chrissy's co-guardian with Rick like we discussed. No more calls about what's best for Chrissy when I don't even know what's best for me. After I hang up with you, I'm leaving with Anthony and no one, not even you, will be able to find me or reach me. I know you always do what's best for Chrissy, so I couldn't live with myself if I left without telling you what's really going on here. Rick lets Chrissy visit with Dad. He doesn't care about the court order. He thinks it's fine if Chrissy sees our dad whenever she wants, and there's nothing I can say to change his mind." The probation officer thanked me for letting her know. She was sorry I needed to run but understood the pressure I must be under, and let me know that Chrissy would be taken from Rick's care immediately. Since I was unable to care for Chrissy at the time, she would be placed in foster care. She also let me know that Dad, then out on bail, would be sent back to jail until his sentencing for violating the court order.

Later that day Dad was back in jail and Chrissy was taken into protective custody. When Rick found out I had called Chrissy's probation officer and told her he was allowing Chrissy to see Dad, he was livid. Rick never spoke to me again.

Chapter 12
PATH B

On Monday, January 2, 1984, I arrived a few minutes early for my first appointment with Sharyn. Sitting alone in the tiny waiting room, I felt my stomach knot like it always did when I was nervous. Coming here had seemed like a good idea when I was curled up on the floor in pain, helpless and sobbing beside Dad's photo, wanting only to die. Now, unable to sit still or get comfortable in my hard chair, it seemed like a terrible idea. How could talking to a complete stranger help me?

I stared down at the bare wood floor, trying not to think of Dad awaiting sentencing. I tried to forget how long he might be locked up for. I didn't want to think about how much I still loved him, either. Actually, I didn't want to think of him at all ever again. Of course, the more I tried not to think about my dad, the more I thought about him. I missed him too much, and it was killing me inside.

After a few minutes, Sharyn, a pretty woman with dark wavy hair and light skin, came out and greeted me. She led me down a narrow hallway to her office. I stopped in the doorway, hesitant to enter. "Sorry, Sharyn," I said, "but I don't know if this is such a good idea."

"I'm sorry you feel that way, Lily. May I ask why?" Sharyn looked at me like she genuinely cared and wanted to hear what my concerns were. Dad had looked at me that way too.

"Well, I've never been in therapy before. I don't even know what goes on here. But, if I'm supposed to come in here and blame my parents for all my problems, I'm going home," I said, not sure what to expect, but very sure the blame game wasn't something I wanted to play.

"If that's something you don't want to do," she said, "then we won't do it, okay?" I nodded slowly, surprised at Sharyn's seemingly simple solution.

I walked into her office and stared at the couch. I recalled a movie I had watched in my high school psychology class about Sigmund Freud, the father of psychoanalysis. The movie depicted a typical session in which the patient lay on an oversized couch while Sigmund sat close by, taking notes. He asked the patient questions about her problems and then nodded his head in agreement while saying "uh hum, and how did that make you feel?"—all the while encouraging the patient to continue talking until she eventually answered her own questions and solved her own problems. If therapy was that simple, I thought, I might as well lie down right now and start talking to a wall—same idea. For this Path B to work, I needed a safe, supportive place where I could ask whatever questions I had and get answers. I would not answer my own questions—how silly and useless. "Can I ask questions here?" I asked.

"Of course you can, Lily," Sharyn said, nodding and smiling. She was always smiling. I wondered how long that would last. I didn't tell Sharyn this, but I knew that the first time I asked a question and she was short, impatient, or angry with me or had no answer or asked me to stop asking so many questions, I would bolt.

I sat on the couch. Sharyn told me a little about herself and then asked if I could tell her a little about myself. I told her what life was like when I had lived with my mom, how she had beaten me for as long as I could remember and how I had run away from her and reunited with my dad, and then had an affair with him. I told her about my dad's arrest, about leaving Rick's house, needing to run from the chaos and hide, and how my dad was awaiting sentencing but I didn't know when he would go to prison or for how long because no one in my family knew where I was and I liked it that way. "You sound like you are pretty overwhelmed right now. Would you like me to check into your father's sentencing for you?" she asked. I smiled and nodded. She jotted down some notes while I sat in silence and waited.

"I don't know if I can afford this. I don't have a job," I said.

"It sounds like you qualify for the Victims of Crime (VOC) Program." Sharyn explained that the state of California had a program known as the Victims of Crime (VOC) Program, in which a victim of a crime could receive funds for crime-related expenses. I learned that the VOC Program's primary funding was the Restitution Fund—monies collected through fines and penalties imposed by judges upon persons convicted of crimes in California. My dad was required to pay a restitution fine, and I qualified for the VOC Program. I could use the funds to help pay for my therapy with Sharyn.

For the rest of the session I asked Sharyn lots of questions like why did people come to talk to her and did these people ever get better, and if they did get better, how long did it usually take? I kept waiting for my questions to annoy her, to finally crack her calm façade like they would most people, but they never did.

After my first therapy session, I walked back to my car and sat there staring at my appointment card for the following Thursday, wondering if I could really trust Sharyn. In the end, was she only going to hurt me? Was Path B just a complete waste of time—and Path A my only viable choice?

———

For the next two months Sharyn and I met weekly. During this time, I opened up to Sharyn even more about my mom's abuse. When I was growing up, my mom's favorite game was Break Me. I hated that game, but Mom liked to play it all the time. I had to be very careful because Mom could start playing the game at any time without my knowing, and she always won. We both knew the rules very well— Mom would find what I loved and destroy it. I would try to pretend I didn't love something because Mom was always watching, trying to see what it was that I loved so that she could win the game, so that she could break me. I lived in constant fear of my mom playing her game and winning, leaving me devastated, shattered and broken on the floor.

One of my favorite things to do when I was a little was draw on my chalkboard. I would grab my rainbow colored chalks and disappear into my world of good guys and bad guys, best friends and worst villains.

One summer afternoon when I was six, as Underdog and I were busy battling Simon Bar Sinister, protecting poor helpless Polly, feeling on top of the world as superheroes do, my mom's anger brought me crashing back into her world, leaving mine far behind.

"Lily, what the hell is wrong with you? Why didn't you answer me?" Mom angrily asked.

"I'm sorry, Mommy. I didn't hear you," I replied, frightened.

"What? What do you mean you didn't hear me? I called you five times!" Mom said furiously.

"I was playing," I said nervously.

"Well, I'll teach you what happens when you decide to play instead of listen to your mother. Maybe next time you'll come when I call you!" She slapped me hard across the face several times, but the pain did not compare to the pain I felt as I watched my mom destroy my chalkboard, kicking and stomping on it with her foot until it broke into pieces.

"No! No! No! No Mommy, please! I promise I'll listen next time, but please, Mommy, not my chalkboard!" I begged. But Mom did not listen to my pleas. I had lost the game. Mom won. My spirit was broken. I fell to the floor, destroyed.

Another thing I loved to do when I was a child was listen to my records. One Saturday afternoon I was dancing and singing along to my Dr. Dolittle album out loud, lost in a world where I could converse with animals. Suddenly, the music died. I stopped, dead in my tracks. The joy that once filled my room was now completely gone. Tears filled my eyes. Oh, no! There was only one person who would do that...

"That's it! I've had it!" Mom screamed as she scraped the record player's needle violently across my favorite record, angrily tore it off the turntable, threw my album hard to the floor, and began jumping up and down on it, shattering it into a million pieces. "I've heard enough of this shit! Now you *will* hear me when I call you!"

"No! No! No!" I screamed the only word I had. As I fell to the floor, shattered like my Dr. Dolittle album, I knew my mom had won the Break Me game, again.

And during these games, she would beat me. Each time my mom hit me, I told myself, *When I get big, I'll do it better. I'll hurt better. I'll beat better. I'll cause far more pain than my mommy ever can.* I couldn't wait to be big so that I could finally do what adults do— inflict pain on children. I held on to this belief so tightly that it would be one of the most difficult ones for me to release during my therapy work. Knowing the harm I wanted to inflict now that I was an adult was a big reason I never wanted to have children. I didn't trust myself.

Sharyn explained that this was a perfect example of how the cycle of abuse works. "Your mom was just doing to you what was done to her, and if you weren't here, determined to break the cycle of abuse, you would most likely go on to abuse your future children." It was sad to me how easily abuse passed from generation to generation, and sadder still how difficult it was to stop.

I stared at the books on Sharyn's shelves, trying not to cry. "Sometimes I have flashbacks of my mom hitting me. And sometimes when I hear her voice on the phone or am around her I start to feel really anxious."

Sharyn said flashbacks and anxiety were common symptoms of a condition called post-traumatic stress disorder (PTSD). We discussed PTSD and how a soldier in combat and a child like me living in constant fear of being hit or hurt can suffer from PTSD as a result of his or her traumatic experiences. Soon after, I was diagnosed with PTSD.

"Did your dad molest you?" Sharyn asked.

"No, my dad never molested me. My stepfather Carlos molested me when I was eleven. I was sixteen when I had sex with my dad, and I wanted to." Sharyn felt my father had molested me because even at sixteen, I was still a child and my father was the adult who had all the power in our relationship. But I disagreed. Naïvely, I thought she didn't understand me or my dad like I did.

While it was somewhat uncomfortable to talk to Sharyn about having sex with my dad, I really didn't have much shame about it. I had loved my dad very much and for the most part enjoyed the sex and didn't feel what we were doing was wrong. I didn't care much what Sharyn thought about it either. But there were things I had done that I was very, very ashamed of, things only my dad knew about. Each week I learned to trust Sharyn a little more, always testing her, telling her things I used to tell only my dad.

My dad had done terrible things that he would never see as wrong, but he also knew the horrible things I had done and didn't judge me—he just wrapped me in his arms and held me. That was the closest thing to unconditional love I had ever had. He never made me feel ashamed for anything I had done, and that was good because I felt like I had enough shame and guilt for the both of us. But Dad was in prison now, and I wanted to trust Sharyn like I had my dad.

During one session, I sat shaking with sweaty palms, my stomach knotting. I was sure once Sharyn heard what I had to say, she would be shocked and so repulsed by the sight of me that she would ask me to leave. She would say I was beyond her help, finally seeing me as I saw myself. "When I was six, I beat little kittens. I beat them and beat them with a ping pong paddle until they cried, and I liked it. I liked it a lot. So, Sharyn, what do you think of me now?" I could still hear the cries of the terrified kittens, still see them fleeing from me. I felt the shame of what I had done seventeen years before wash over me, but I pushed it away. I remembered Dad's arms wrapped around me, rocking me gently as I cried when, at seventeen, I told him what I had done. I knew I was screwed up, and now Sharyn would know too.

"Well, Lily, I think you were a smart child who made a very wise choice," Sharyn said.

"What? Why?" I asked, shocked by her response. I reached for a tissue. Even though I didn't understand what she was saying, I wanted to know more.

"Because, you were an innocent six-year-old child who felt powerless and who had to make a choice to either be a victim or a perpetrator, and you decided you didn't want to be a victim anymore." Sharyn went on to explain why hurting kittens made perfect sense for a child like me who was a victim of physical and emotional abuse and who had learned violence. I had desperately needed to feel powerful. When Sharyn explained why I'd done what I had with the kittens, and when I understood, I felt my shame slowly melt away. I finally felt safe with her.

From then on, I trusted Sharyn completely. I knew there was nothing I could tell her that would make her love or understand me any less. She was like the parent I'd always wished for.

Chapter 13
DAD GOES TO PRISON

"Lily," Sharyn said during our tenth session, "I thought you should know that your dad was found guilty of lewd and lascivious conduct upon a child and incest. He was sent to Vacaville State Prison last week for six years and eight months." My heart sank into the pit of my stomach. I had known for months that my dad was going to be sent to prison, but now it was real. He was there. I struggled with the thought of my dad sitting in a prison cell, alone. I wondered what he thought about. Did he think of me? Was he mad at me? Did he hate me?

Right after my session with Sharyn, I ran down to the courthouse and got a copy of my dad's file, then sat in my car, lit a cigarette, and began reading the court report by the criminal evaluator who was assigned to my dad's case.

I found the criminal evaluator's report extremely insightful. She stated: *"...[Bill Capello's] family of origin is one which is so fraught with serious sexually aberrant behavior that it is not a surprise that he came to be involved in similar behavior.*

Psychological examinations reveal that he not only demonstrates a strong defense system to deal with his behavior, but also that he is insensitive to the effect of his behavior upon his victims...it is felt that defendant would not at this time be appropriate for the Parents United Program...

The Capello family system is one which, on some level, accepts as normal, behavior which is socially unacceptable. The children have been exposed to in-family incest, homosexual acting out and pedophilic behavior. The line between normal and abnormal has been crossed on such a regular basis that it is difficult for them at times to distinguish between the two...

Keeping the family intact may have some value, however breaking the family system as it exists today is far more necessary at this time...Mr. Capello could benefit from behavioral aversive conditioning. Given the degree of molestation and the suggestion of additional pedophilic activity, it is this writer's opinion that defendant is in need of therapy in a program in which he could be supervised at all times and one which he could not verbally manipulate his way around...

Without this plan being implemented, and if the court were to send defendant directly to state prison, the family would be so devastated that they would most likely cling to anything familiar to them (i.e. aberrant behavior), they would most likely become molesters themselves or allow their own children to be molested (the molest cycle). Once their father was returned from prison, they would most likely reunite and in some way re-enact old behavior patterns..."

In an ideal world, Dad's attending aversive therapy was clearly the perfect plan for us all, but in reality Dad had no interest in changing his ways. Dad was given the opportunity for treatment at Atascadero State Hospital, but when he learned it did not result in a reduced sentence, he declined and was sent directly to Vacaville State Prison.

I sat there, staring at the report in disbelief. The incest, the denial, the molest cycle—sometimes I couldn't even believe this was my family. I put the report down and cried.

———

That weekend Anthony and I drove up to Pocatello, Idaho, to visit my mom. My mom and I had been communicating, and I wanted to try to build a closer relationship with her. After driving nearly fourteen hours, we located Mom's house, a charming two-story home on a nice, quiet street. Anthony parked the car under the carport next to a large stack of firewood. Inside, we visited with my mom and her sixth husband Juan, a short and stocky man with a thin mustache and glasses.

While Juan, Anthony, Bart, and Cindy played basketball in the backyard, I talked with Mom. "My dad got sentenced this week for molesting kids. He's in Vacaville now," I said.

"See, Lily," Mom said, "I told you he was a child molester, remember?"

"Yeah, I remember. You were right, Mom." I didn't want to argue with her. Mom smiled, happy I finally knew what she knew. But I really didn't. I knew she was thinking about her accusations that my dad had molested me in the bathtub when I was a year and a half old. Dad had said he was just washing me, and I refused to believe it had happened any differently. It was as if I couldn't go there, couldn't open that door. I wasn't ready then.

"It's been really hard though, Mom. I miss my dad," I looked down at the floor trying not to cry.

"Why? He is a terrible, terrible man," she looked at me, confused. I wanted her to understand, but she never did.

"I brought the statement I gave to the police with me. It was very hard for me to write. Do you want to read it?"

"Okay," she said. I handed her the report. She sat in her chair and began reading, her glasses perched low on her nose. I sat down next to her on the floor leaned up against her legs, watching her read. She still smelled like cigarettes and White Shoulders.

Mom looked at me over her glasses, shocked. "Lily, how could you sleep with your own father?"

"I loved him, Mom," I said. She stared at me, judging me. I felt that if I weren't her daughter she would have thrown me out like trash. Of course she wouldn't understand me. She never had before, why would she now?

After my mom finished reading my statement, I blurted out, "I'm seeing a therapist," then immediately wished I hadn't. Mom glared at me. She didn't like therapists. Growing up, she had always said we should never tell anyone anything about what happened in our family, that it was private and wasn't anyone's business. So I hadn't, until now.

"Why?" she asked as she lit a cigarette.

"To help me get better," I said. There was an awkward silence. "You know, living with my dad really messed me up." Mom nodded, looking relieved. I was too scared to tell her that living with her all those years had really messed me up too. She wouldn't have understood anyway. After all, she never did anything wrong. I left feeling closer to my mom, but sad and disappointed she didn't at least try to understand the relationship I'd had with my dad.

On October 13, 1984, seven months after Dad had been sent to prison, Anthony and I got married. Anthony was twenty-six and I was twenty-three. We'd been together almost three years and felt ready to give marriage a try.

Mom got a minister to perform our ceremony in her home. Mom, Juan, Bart, Cindy, Eileen, and Todd were in attendance. I wore a simple white gown and Anthony rented a light blue tux. Next, we headed over to Jackpot, Nevada, and spent our honeymoon night in a fancy tower suite in Cactus Pete's. Mom had stocked our room with treats: strawberries dipped in chocolate, a bottle of champagne, and a bottle of Mr. Bubbles conveniently placed next to our huge private Jacuzzi. In the morning, Anthony and I enjoyed a buffet breakfast in the Canyon Cove Buffet with Mom and Juan. I found it fun to make my way through the buffet lines, piled my plate high with food and then hurry back, grab the thick black crayon, and mark my lucky numbers before the Keno runner made it to our table. Anthony got lucky and won a couple hundred dollars on his Keno ticket, so Mom said Anthony should treat for breakfast, which he did.

A week after our wedding, Anthony and I left for our honeymoon. We spent ten days in Maui walking along the white sandy beaches, driving the beautiful, winding road to Hana, and soaking in the sun. It was everything I had ever dreamed of.

When we returned home, I found a letter from my dad waiting for me. Too afraid to open it, I sat for almost ten minutes just staring at the envelope. Why was he writing me a letter now, after all this time? I took a deep breath and, with shaking hands and a pounding heart, tore open the envelope.

> *Dear Lily,*
>
> *I trust this letter finds you in good health.*
>
> *I want to thank you for turning me in. I realize how hard it must have been.*
>
> *I am asking for your forgiveness as I realize how very wrong I was in the relationship with you.*
>
> *I am very concerned about where the future of you and Chrissy will be, I hope you are making progress in your counseling and I hope Chrissy is receiving help also.*
>
> *I hope you will find it in your heart to forgive me. Do you feel up to writing me? If you do, then by all means, go and get yourself a pen and a piece of paper, and jot down any and all questions, and send them to me, and I will send you answers, as best I can. I hope that you can find the time and have the energy to write me. I will type any and all answers to your inquiries, mainly because I sit in an office and my*

job pertains to typing and therefore all the paper and envelopes are free. No the stamps are not free! I have been working as a clerk since I arrived here. I am up to about 45-55 words per minute. Not bad for 2 fingers, eh? I have been receiving quite a few letters, so besides doing office work, I get a lot of practice.

I will now tell you a little about what I am doing. I am living in a triple wide trailer, converted into a dorm. Twenty five, (25) to a dorm. My brother sent me a 13" color TV a few weeks ago, and so I watch a lot of football, baseball play-offs and the new TV shows. Of course the Johnny Carson and Bizarre are a favorite at the late hours, however some of the new shows are pretty neat. Are there any new ones you watch? Sure makes the time go by fast. Well, faster than reading books.

Well, I will close for now. Hope to hear from you, however if you don't feel up to answering at this time, I understand.

Yours Always,

Dad

PS Give Gumdrop a hug or kiss as you see appropriate.

PSS Have a Happy Thanksgiving!!!

My emotions were all over the map. I wanted to go to Vacaville, hug him, tell him I forgave him, and then sit in front of his thirteen-inch color TV and watch Johnny Carson like we used to, as if nothing had happened. I still wanted a normal dad. But at the same time I hated him for everything he had done and never wanted to speak to him again. I was devastated because I knew he could never be just a normal dad.

My mind flooded with questions I wanted my dad to answer. How could you molest kids, Dad? How many kids did you molest? How could you cheat on me? How many times did you cheat? Was it easy for you to lie to me? Did you ever love me Dad? You know, like the way I loved you?

I wasn't sure if I could forgive him. My stomach began to hurt, and I thought I could feel my heart breaking. I ran to the bathroom and got sick.

Later, I sat down and tried to write a letter to my dad, but I couldn't. Part of me desperately wanted to write back, but deep down I somehow knew I had to cut him off completely in order to get better. At first I thought I *had* to write back because he was my father. I thought I didn't have a choice. It was Sharyn who gave me permission not to write my dad if I wasn't ready. Relieved, I never wrote back to him.

For the next several months, I thought long and hard about my relationship with my dad. I was torn. On one hand, I still loved my dad very much, but on the other hand, I was worried he'd lie to me, manipulate me, and hurt me all over again. I feared that what Art had said about my dad was true. Dad could not be helped, and he would molest again. I thought about how I would feel if I ever did have a child one day, and my dad molested him or her. Or if I found out my dad molested a friend's child because I had introduced him to that friend. As much as I still loved him, would I really be okay with helping my dad find his next victim? At that moment, I broke into tears because I knew my answer. I would never talk to my dad again.

Chapter 14
LIL

In April 1985, over a year into our therapy, Sharyn and I started talking about my inner child. Sharyn said whether we're aware of it or not, the little child we once were still lives in us today, affecting everything we feel and do. Lately, I hadn't been sleeping well. I kept having nightmares about my mom. She was holding the gun to her head, threatening to pull the trigger like she had twelve years before. Sharyn said my inner child was stuck in the past, scared and reliving that terrifying day over and over again. To stop the nightmares and begin the healing process, I needed to find her, rescue her, and let her know she was safe now. I said that didn't make a whole lot of sense because I was pretty sure I didn't have a little kid inside of me. Still, I was curious and wanted to either find my elusive inner child and put an end to these terrifying nightmares or prove to Sharyn that I'd never had one in the first place.

I got comfortable on Sharyn's couch, closed my eyes, and took a few deep breaths to calm myself, thinking that if I really did have an inner child, I didn't want to leave her lost all alone somewhere inside me. But when Sharyn invited me to turn my attention inward, I couldn't. There was something spinning inside me, trying to grab me and throw me somewhere else. It felt like I was being sucked up into a tornado. Before I could scream, it picked me up and slammed me against the far wall of Sharyn's office. I immediately opened my eyes in panic, vowing never to try that again. Sharyn calmed me down and let me know it was okay, part of me just wasn't ready yet.

After waiting several weeks, I tried to find my inner child again. Unfortunately, the second attempt to find my inner child ended like the first, with the same tornado waiting for me, again picking me up and slamming me against the wall.

But I didn't give up. The following week I was back on Sharyn's couch with my eyes closed, trying to ignore my racing heart and sweaty palms. I hoped this visualization to find my inner child would not end like the previous two. As I listened to Sharyn's gentle soothing voice, guiding me, calming me, I was relieved there wasn't a tornado waiting for me again. "I don't see anything. It's pitch black in here," I said.

My next step was to envision taking a source of light with me to illuminate the pitch-black darkness within. I visualized flashlights, spotlights, floodlights—brighter and more intense beams of light— and brought these sources of light with me in the hope of seeing something, anything other than the gloomy blackness.

Finally, after six or seven attempts that session, I thought I could see something in the distance. "Wait, I think I see something," I said, as I visualized a strong floodlight in my hand.

"What do you see, Lily?"

"I see an old English street lamp lighting up all this darkness, and beneath it a big cage."

"Is there something in the cage?"

"Yes, it looks like some sort of wild beast is locked up in there. The thing is thrashing about trying to escape, throwing itself violently against the cage bars and howling in pain."

"What does it look like?"

"I can't see its face, but its fur is brown and matted and full of blood. It looks kind of scary." Suddenly the beast collapsed, curling up in the far corner of the cage. As I walked closer, it slowly turned and looked up at me. "Wait. I can finally see its face, Sharyn, and it doesn't look like any beast I've ever seen," I said, trembling. "Its face looks like a child's face. It looks like...it looks like me!" Shocked and confused, I opened my eyes and looked at Sharyn. "Is she my inner child?" I asked, wondering why she looked more like an animal than a child.

"That's a good question. I don't know. Can you ask her what her name is?"

"Okay, I'll try." I closed my eyes and in my mind asked her, "Are you Lily?"

"My name is Lil, not Lily," she barked. She seemed angry and a little scared. *Great,* I thought. *Not only does she look more like an animal than a child, but she has an attitude too.*

"Why do you have fur?" I asked.

"Because Mommy treats her pets far better than me, so I thought she would treat me better if I was an animal too!" I smiled at Lil. What a smart kid she was to become part animal in the hopes that Mom would forget she was a human child, forget she hated her so intensely, and stop yelling at and beating her. Also, the fur conveniently buried and hid Lil's bruises from plain sight so that it was easier for her to forget about them. Lil wished the fur could somehow bury and hide all the hateful, painful words too, so they wouldn't hurt so much.

"I hate my body! So I covered it in fur!" Lil said, but she refused to say why. (I wouldn't find out why until nearly three and a half years later.)

Over the next few months, I got to know my inner child better, and my nightmares of my mom holding a gun to her head lessened. At first I had no real connection with Lil. I'd close my eyes and try to picture her, but I couldn't always see her. Sharyn suggested I find a picture of myself when I was little to help me remember. Flipping through my dad's old photo album, the one I had taken when he was first arrested, I came across a photo of me when I was two years old, dressed in pink and smiling.

That night I stared at the photo, then closed my eyes and tried to visualize my inner child. I finally found her curled up in a corner, crying. Part of me didn't want to get near her. With all that matted fur, she was ugly. And I was afraid to feel her pain. But I couldn't just leave her there like that. So I scooped her up and tried to comfort her. "Shh...it's okay, Lil. I'm here. You're safe now. I won't let anything bad happen to you—I promise."

Even though I did my best to comfort her, Lil still seemed so sad, and I had no idea why or what I should do. Sharyn reminded me how much kids love to play, so I took my inner child to play. Visualizing Lil right there next to me, I went outside and blew bubbles with her. The next day I pictured her as I swung on some swings at the nearby park, and then I dropped by the local pet store to pet a few bunnies. A couple days later I turned on the radio and visualized her singing songs and dancing right there with me. I was having so much fun being with her. It was like being a kid again. I quickly learned that when Lil was happy, so was I.

It took my inner child about five months to trust me enough to feel safe and shed all her fur. She finally believed me when I promised her that I would never let anyone hurt her again. She knew she didn't have to worry anymore that she would be locked away in a cage. She finally trusted that, unlike other people in our past, I was honest and would always keep my word.

Underneath all that fur I'd found a scared and sad little girl who was brave enough to try again. I didn't realize then how much I needed her, how incomplete I had been without her. Without her, I couldn't overcome my past and heal.

An important part of healing my wounded inner child was to be the nurturing parent she had never had. I tried to model myself after Sharyn. Sharyn was like a good parent, the best parent I had ever known, and I wanted to parent Lil like Sharyn had parented me, with lots of love, acceptance, and encouragement. Sharyn always made it look so easy, but it was a lot harder than I thought it would be.

Soon after Lil shed her fur, I began suffering from awful night terrors. I would suddenly wake up trembling, terrified my dad had somehow gotten into my room, wanting to kill me for sending him to prison. I had never felt more guilty or scared in my life. Little Lil was scared for the same reason I was. Closing my eyes, I pictured holding her, trying to comfort her like I imagined Sharyn would, but there was nothing I could do for her, which frustrated me to no end. Part of me started to think being a parent to Lil was too hard and not worth it. I didn't want to feel her terror; I could barely handle my own. I thought maybe I should just toss her right back in that cage where I'd found her. Sometimes life seemed far easier without her.

Sharyn suggested I go shopping and let Lil choose something that would help her to feel safe at night. And it needed to be all her decision, not mine. Sharyn said, "You know Lily, you just might find that as Lil begins to feel safe, so will you." Sometimes I thought Sharyn's ideas were crazy, but I didn't have any better ones. So, I took my inner kid shopping, aware of her as we browsed through store after store. In the fifth store, as we wandered through the stuffed animal section, I suddenly felt her jumping up and down inside of me to catch my attention. I stopped and looked up. There peering over the top shelf was a huge three-foot-long lion. Instantly I knew she had found what she was looking for.

That night the lion lay in bed facing the door, keeping guard over his scared little Lil as I held him tightly with the nightlight on. Lil felt a little bit safer believing her lion wouldn't hesitate to kill her dad to protect her. For the first time in weeks, I slept soundly the whole night through.

Over the next several years in therapy I continued to learn a lot from my inner child work. Now that I had a connection with my inner child, I also had a connection to my feelings of fear and anger, and my past traumas. Each night I would talk to my inner child and try my best to comfort her. It wasn't always easy. Sometimes her pain, which was now my pain too, was so intense that it was only a matter of time before I had to open my eyes, abruptly ending our connection. Then I'd wait until I felt ready to be with her again. But I kept at it. I knew that I could not abandon her now and that I needed her in order to heal.

I learned how to love and accept my inner child Lil just as she was. She was perfect, matted fur and all. Most days I really liked her, too. I had found not only my inner child, but also my inner parent.

At first my inner parent sounded exactly like my mom. When I listened to the inner dialogue between me and my inner child, I could hear my mom's same constant criticism, put-downs, and mean comments coming from me. It made me feel sick to think I was saying the same things to my inner child that my mom had said to me, the same things that had made me feel like I was worthless. So anytime I heard myself sounding like my mom, I stopped. Over time I replaced those negative Mom tapes playing in my head with nicer, more nurturing ones.

Another way I became a good parent to my inner child was by going back to times when I was being abused by my mom, times when I'd felt scared and alone, and rewriting my script in such a way that I was Lil's hero. For instance, I closed my eyes and focused on the gun incident that had happened when I was twelve, but instead of allowing my mom to terrorize me like she had then, I visualized stepping in and stopping her. I took the gun from her hand and said, "Stop it Mom! Now! You're scaring me!" I looked down at Lil crying on the floor and said, "You don't have to be scared anymore, Lil. I'm getting you out of here." Then I helped her up off the floor, put my arm around her shoulder, and walked with her right out of that kitchen.

After doing this guided visualization with Sharyn, the nightmares I'd had about that terrible gun incident ended. I felt so much better about myself, less like a victim and more like someone who was ready to move on and live my life free from fear.

Although my childhood did not change, the way I viewed it did. After rescuing my scared little girl, who had been stuck in the past, I was no longer stuck in the past. In my mind I had stood up for myself and had taken my power back. I was no longer afraid. It was like my mom no longer had the power to terrorize me.

I used to think my dad was the only person who really understood and loved me, but now I knew no one could understand or love my wounded little girl better than I. My love was real, too—no lies, no cons, no conditions and manipulations, just pure, unconditional love and acceptance. There was no longer any need for me to look outside myself for love. With no more nightmares or flashbacks of my mom abusing me, I felt stronger and far better than I ever had before. I believed I was completely healed. Sometimes I even believed I knew everything I needed to know. But I had no idea of the big challenges I still had to face, and all the things I still needed to uncover.

Chapter 15
MR. ZANSKI

One late winter morning Chrissy, now nearly sixteen years old, called to tell me that she had run away from her last foster home because she was being molested there. She had no money and no place to go. I felt bad for her. So, Anthony and I made her an offer. She could come live with us. We would pay for everything—food, clothing, shelter—even college and therapy sessions with Sharyn. Anthony and I wanted Chrissy to have a place she could feel safe and loved and call home. But there was one condition: she would have to stop talking to Dad. As painful as it was, I had stopped talking to Dad, and Chrissy would need to also. I didn't think Chrissy would ever get better if she continued to talk to Dad. I thought he'd use her and possibly even abuse her again. I also didn't want my dad to have access to me or my family and friends once he was released from prison.

"Sorry, Lily, but I could never stop talking to Dad," Chrissy said.

"Okay, Chrissy, I understand. I wish we could help you out. I know it would be really good for you to be here with us. But since you're not strong enough to end it with Dad, we can't help you. So please don't call me again unless you change your mind."

"Okay, but I really don't understand why you'd treat our dad like that. He's doing his time for what he's done wrong. Isn't that good enough for you?"

"No, it's not good enough. I don't believe Dad will ever change. He'll always molest kids and manipulate you and me if given the chance. So, be careful, watch your back, and good luck. I love you." Anthony and I sent Chrissy a few hundred dollars to help her out and wished her all the best.

In the spring of 1987, Dad was released from Vacaville State Prison after serving three years and four months of his six years and eight months sentence. Dad moved to a quiet unit in the Waterloo Apartments on English Drive in San Jose. A week later sixteen-year-old Chrissy moved in with Dad. Of course contact with, let alone living with, Chrissy was a violation of Dad's parole, but as far as Dad and Chrissy were concerned, the authorities would never need to know. It would be their secret. Years later Chrissy described what life was like living with Dad in the Waterloo Apartments.

Dad had given Chrissy his new address soon after moving in. A few days later Chrissy knocked on Dad's door. She felt nervous to see him again. Suddenly he opened the door.

"Well hello, Chrissy, let me take a look at you," Dad said. It had been over three years since he had seen his youngest daughter.

"Sure, whatever," Chrissy replied. Living on the streets had really toughened her up.

"You've grown so much since I last saw you," Dad observed. He then hugged Chrissy. "I'm so sorry you've had such a hard time. I've missed you."

"Yeah, I've missed you too," Chrissy said as she hugged Dad back.

"Well, this must feel awkward being here with me. It's been over three years," Dad said.

"Yeah, it sorta sucks when your dad goes to prison for fucking kids," Chrissy replied in her direct, no-nonsense manner.

"You're right. I agree. What I've done does suck. So, what can I do to make you feel more comfortable living here with me?" Dad asked.

"How 'bout putting a fucking lock on my bedroom door so I don't have to worry about you sneaking into my room late at night," Chrissy demanded.

"Done," Dad replied, and that night Chrissy had a lock on her bedroom door.

The following week, a friend of Dad's got him a job in the payroll department of her company. Dad quickly learned everything there was to know about payroll. In February of the following year, Dad set up a fictitious company. He rented a suite and opened a business account at Bank of America under a nonexistent company name. He subsequently cashed payroll checks issued by the made-up company at various Mr. Cash check cashing stations. Of course, each check was returned for nonsufficient funds, but by that time Dad, with his false names and disguises, along with the fictitious company, was long gone.

Also during that time, Dad became friends with his next-door neighbors, Alice, a quiet and kind lady who had recently separated from her husband Stan, and Luther, her curly blonde-haired, blue-eyed nine-year-old son. It turned out that Alice was looking for someone to babysit her son after school and during the upcoming winter break, and Dad was more than happy to help her out. In December, Dad watched Luther at his apartment.

One Monday afternoon, Chrissy came home after spending the weekend hanging out with her girlfriends. As she opened the front door, Chrissy heard a familiar voice saying, "I know you are, but what am I?" followed by, "Arrggh!" *What the fuck?* Chrissy thought. She ran down the hall to her bedroom. When she flung open the door, she saw Luther sitting on the floor playing with her beloved Pee-wee Herman doll.

"Hey, Luther, give me that right now!" Chrissy demanded. She had become very attached to her Pee-wee Herman doll, dressed in a size-too-small 1950's style gray plaid suit with a skinny red bowtie, which she had stolen two years before.

"No," Luther responded as he threw a mini temper tantrum while hugging his newfound toy tightly. He was an only child, accustomed to getting what he wanted, and he wanted Pee-wee.

What a spoiled brat, Chrissy thought. *And why's this kid here anyway? He shouldn't be here. What the fuck's Dad doing?* Chrissy wondered. She felt a knot tighten in her stomach. Chrissy found Dad in the living room watching TV and asked him, "Why's Luther here?"

Dad calmly replied, "Oh, his Mom asked if I could babysit, and I told her sure, no problem." Chrissy didn't say a word, even though she wanted to. She sensed something was very wrong, but things were going well between her and Dad and she didn't want to ruin that, so she bit her tongue. She patiently waited until Luther put Pee-wee down. Then she grabbed her doll and her stash of weed and left.

Luther saw his dad, Stan, on New Year's Eve. They had a good relationship, and Luther told his dad that his neighbor Bill had touched him sexually. Stan believed his son and was furious.

One January morning, Stan came to Dad's apartment. He told Chrissy that once he found our dad, he would kick his ass for touching his boy. Chrissy met up with Dad at a friend's house, told him what Stan had said, and asked him, "What the fuck's going on?"

"Oh, Chrissy, I didn't touch Luther. Luther told me his dad's been touching and fondling him, doing inappropriate things Luther doesn't like. He's just a confused little boy saying I'm touching him when the sad truth is it's his own dad that's doing all the touching," Dad said as he shook his head. A sad expression settled upon his face.

Luther's dad never did get the chance to confront my dad because Dad spent far less time at the apartment in fear of him. But Stan did contact the police the following week and filed charges against my dad. In addition, charges were filed against my dad for setting up the fictitious company and cashing bad checks at various Mr. Cash check cashing stations.

The following April, eleven months after he'd been released from Vacaville State Prison, Dad was indicted for child molestation and grand theft. With the help of a good attorney, Dad was found not guilty in the molestation case, but he was found guilty of grand theft and sentenced to one year in the county jail. A scared Chrissy fled the Waterloo Apartments and moved with a friend to Arizona.

That same year Sharyn encouraged me to go to college. Once there, not only did I get to prove to myself that I was smart after being told my whole life by my mom that I was stupid—actually getting A's if I studied hard—but here no one knew me or my past. And I didn't want anyone to know. I wanted a fresh start. So, I refused to think about my dad anymore. I was done. We were over. As far as I was concerned, my dad was no longer my father. And if anyone asked me about my father, I would either tell them about my wonderful dad Jeffrey who lived in England, whom I'd reconnected with when my dad went to prison, or I would tell them about my mom's latest husband. But I never told anyone about my biological father, the one I'd had an affair with, the sociopath, the sexual predator now sitting in prison.

I had never taken a chemistry course in high school, so I enrolled in the entry-level chemistry class offered at my local community college. A tall thin man walked in the classroom. I didn't know what it was about him. Maybe it was his mischievous, mysterious smile, or maybe it was the way his eyes seemed to look right through me, but I immediately wanted him. I sat up straight in my chair and watched him. He wrote his name along with the name of the course on the chalkboard. "Hello, class, my name is Mr. Zanski. How's everyone doing today?"

"Good," I said, as did most of the class.

"This is Chem 25, Fundamentals of Chemistry," he said, and as he turned to underline the course title on the board three times for emphasis, I couldn't help but stare at his firm behind. "Just in case you weren't sure if you're sitting in the right class or not," he said grinning sarcastically.

He pulled his overhead projector closer to the class, flipped it on, and started going over some of the things we would be covering in his class like the different states of matter—solids, liquids, and gases. "So class, if H_2O is the formula for water, then what is the formula for ice?" he asked, looking around the classroom with a huge smile on his face. He had the cutest dimples and biggest brown eyes I had ever seen. I heard the students around me mumbling and shifting in their seats. I turned to my plump classmate Pam sitting next to me. We looked at each other puzzled and shrugged. "H_2O cubed, of course," he said, laughing loudly. His stupid jokes made me laugh. I felt at ease in his class right away.

Later that day, as Pam and I ate lunch, I asked her, "So Pam, what do you think of our chemistry professor?" wondering if her heart skipped a beat like mine did whenever he was near.

"Oh my God, Lily," she said shaking her head, "I tell you, there's something very, very wrong with that man. He's really creepy, you know?" I shrugged. "He's sick and disgusting. He turns my stomach. Did you know that he was fired from here for inappropriate behavior with one of his students?" Being the dean's secretary, Pam had the inside scoop about many things, including our teacher.

"No, I didn't know that." But it gave me hope that he might be inappropriate with me too. "So, if he was fired for something like that, then why is he back here teaching?" I asked intrigued, trying to look concerned and disgusted like Pam was.

"I don't know how he managed to get rehired," Pam said as she pushed up her glasses. "But I bet whatever he did was something sneaky and underhanded." I nodded and then took a long sip of my soda. She continued. "You know, if I didn't need this class to graduate, I would never be anywhere near a class Zanski was teaching, ever!" I nodded again and looked down at my half-eaten sandwich. There really was nothing she could possibly say that would make me want to turn and run from Mr. Zanski. If anything, the more she talked about how horrible he was, the more appealing he became to me.

In class I'd sit in the front row next to Pam where I could see everything and listen carefully to Mr. Zanski's lectures. I tried my best not to be distracted by Mr. Zanski, but sometimes the only chemistry I could think about was the one I wanted between us.

Two weeks later, Pam and I ran into our classmate Brenda, a long-legged brunette, in the hallway. "You two won't believe what just happened!" Brenda said.

"What?" Pam and I asked in unison.

"I've really been struggling with our chemistry homework. So, earlier today I went to Mr. Zanski's office for help. He was trying to explain to me how to do some density problem, and I wasn't getting it. Then he says, 'Hey, Brenda, no worries. I know an easy way for you to get an A,' and he leans over and tries to kiss me. Yuck! What an asshole!"

"Oh, Brenda, that's terrible. I'm so sorry," Pam said as I looked down and shook my head, pretending to be disgusted. "You know, I was just telling Lily the other day what a sick, sick man he is, wasn't I Lily?"

"Yeah, you sure were," I said.

"So, are you going to report him, Brenda?" Pam asked. "You really should, you know. It's not like they won't believe you. He's done this sort of thing before. And I'm sure they'd fire him immediately and never let him teach here again or anywhere else for that matter. His teaching days would be over."

"Yeah, you really should report him, Brenda," I said, hoping she wouldn't. I studied Brenda, trying to figure out what she had that I didn't. Why was Mr. Zanski hitting on her and not me? I'd gone to his office a couple of times and he never tried anything like that on me. I found myself becoming more and more jealous of his inappropriate advances toward Brenda. I really wanted him to notice and make his moves on me instead.

"Yeah, I know I should report him. I really should," Brenda said sighing. "But the thing is I don't want to go through a messy 'he said/she said' confrontation, or worse. I just want to pass this class and move on."

Angry that Mr. Zanski had hit on Brenda and not me, I was determined to get him to notice me. Over the next few weeks I attempted to flirt and turn on every possible charm I had so that even Mr. Zanski couldn't resist. I made it a point to get to school early and stay after class late, and dropped by his office unannounced, holding out hope that he would be inappropriate with me too. But he never was, and this made me feel even more frustrated and angry.

For a moment I wondered if I had lost my mind to be willing to throw away my happy life with Anthony for this guy. I knew deep down that life with Mr. Zanski could only bring me heartache and misery, but I didn't care. I had to have him.

One afternoon, feeling desperate, I waited from a safe distance for Mr. Zanski to leave his last class of the day. I knew his routine—he would walk in my direction on the way to the parking lot where he would get into his car and drive home. I would walk in the opposite direction and make it look like we'd run into each other by chance. If I executed it perfectly, I would be walking with my head down, looking totally engrossed in something far more important than he, and I would "accidentally" collide into him. My books would fall to the ground and we would brush up against each other as we both leaned over to collect them. Then he would suddenly realize just how much he wanted me.

After twenty minutes, all of his students had slowly dispersed and

I could see Mr. Zanski walking in my direction. With my head down and books in tow, I started walking in his direction when suddenly I lost my nerve and quickly started walking the other way.

"Hey, is that you, Lily?" I heard him ask, stopping me dead in my tracks.

I slowly looked up. "Oh...hey...Mr. Zanski. Fancy meeting you here. What's up?" I said, trying to look surprised.

"Oh, I'm heading home. It's been a long day. You?" he asked as he waved to a few students passing by.

"Uh, yeah, I'll be heading home soon, too," I said.

"Did you enjoy the lecture today?" he asked.

"Uh, yeah, I guess," I said. Then he started talking about chemistry, the last thing I wanted to talk about. I wanted to hear how much he wanted me, how he couldn't resist me. I wanted him to tell me that I was all he ever thought about, and even though he knew it was wrong for a teacher to date his student, he loved me so much that he didn't care and that being with me was worth losing his job for. Lastly, I wanted to hear him say that he had made a huge mistake. Brenda was not the woman for him, I was.

As we stood there making small talk, not only wasn't he saying anything I wanted to hear, but I was starting to get the feeling he wasn't even interested in me. When I thought about how he probably saw me as far less attractive than Brenda, I could feel my blood boil. What I really wanted to do was excuse myself from our stupid conversation and walk over to the women's restroom to write my suicide note in which all the blame for ending my life fell directly on him for not loving me. I mean, couldn't he see the insufferable pain he was causing me? Didn't he know that I didn't want to live if he didn't love me back because to me that meant I was worthless? I wanted him to never forget how he had driven me to suicide. And I wanted him to never forget me. I walked away.

The following Monday, as I stood outside the classroom waiting for Mr. Zanski to open the door, I felt an enormous pressure building in my stomach, like it was going to explode. Looking down, I waited to see my belly rip wide open, blood and internal organs bursting out because I was sure no mere skin could possibly withstand all that pressure without tearing. "Good morning, Lily," Mr. Zanski said, flashing me a dazzling smile as he unlocked the door. Trying to hide my pain, I somehow managed to smile back. Then I ran to my seat, hoping that my stomach would either stop aching or explode already.

As I sat there in the front row listening to Mr. Zanski's lecture about the colligative properties of solutions and trying to ignore my aching stomach and not be sick, I could feel myself starting to leave my body. It felt like I was being sucked up off my seat by a powerful invisible vacuum. Instinctively I held on to my chair tightly, trying not to get lifted off the ground. In my mind I screamed, "No, no! Please! Stop! I don't want to go!" But it was no use. I left my body. Suddenly, I couldn't see anything that was going on around me or hear anything being said in the classroom because I was no longer there. Instead, I was trapped in a dark and lonely void. All I could hear was my own screaming. All I wanted was to be back in class. I wondered if anyone knew I wasn't there, or if anyone cared. I had no idea how much time had passed, but then as quickly as I had left, I was back and the bell was ringing, startling me. I ran out the door.

Pam chased after me. "Lily, what's wrong?"

"What do you mean?" I said, still in shock at what had happened.

"Well, the teacher was asking you what the boiling point was for that solution he had written up on the board, and you didn't say anything. He repeated the question like three times and all you did was hold your pencil and stare off into space. Are you okay?"

"Yeah, I'm okay. Just having a bad day I guess." I dared not tell her the truth—that I had suddenly left my body and was unable to hear or see our teacher. How could I possibly expect her to understand that? I sure as hell didn't. And it scared me to death not knowing if or when it might happen again.

Later that day, as Pam and I ate lunch in the cafeteria, I happened to spot Mr. Zanski sitting alone at a nearby table eating his lunch. I tried not to stare as I pretended I was sitting there with him having lunch, laughing and horsing around. I imagined I was playing footsie with him under the table, letting my foot slowly wander up between his legs. But my fantasy abruptly ended when he stood up and started walking toward us. The closer he got, the faster my heart raced. I looked down at my plate feeling anxious and excited, wondering if he was really going to come over to our table and talk to me. Maybe he finally felt the sparks between us like I did. When I looked up and saw him standing in front of me, smiling, I felt like I was going to leave my body, that same vacuum feeling I'd experienced in class earlier. But I didn't want to leave my body. Not again. I wanted to stay and hear what he had to say. Again I started screaming in my mind, "No, no! Please! Stop! I don't want to go!" Luckily, this time I got to stay, sort of. I could see everything that was going on around me, but I couldn't hear anything. It was like someone had pushed the mute button on the TV remote. I watched in horror as Mr. Zanski's mouth started moving, but there was no sound. Frightened, I knew I had to think of something fast.

All I could do was watch his every move and try to read his body language and facial expressions accurately, then nod and smile back at him at just the right time so that he couldn't tell that I really didn't hear a word he was saying. So I smiled at him and decided to give it my best shot, having my very first conversation as a totally deaf person. When I saw him smile, I smiled. When he nodded, I nodded. It seemed to be working well because I never saw a puzzled look come over his adorable face. After what seemed like an eternity, he turned and walked back to his table. As I took a deep breath, relieved that it was finally over, my hearing suddenly came back.

I looked over at Pam who was finishing up her lunch. "I know you're going to think I'm crazy, but I didn't hear a word he just said."

Pam looked at me confused. But then, like a real friend she said, "No, I don't think you're crazy. Were you just preoccupied or something?"

"Yeah, I guess you could say that," I smiled. "So, could you please tell me what he had to say? I really want to know."

"Well, he said he just finished grading our last test and wanted to congratulate you. You had the highest score in the class." Shocked, I looked over at Mr. Zanski. He raised his water glass to me and mouthed, "Congratulations." I mouthed back, "Thank you."

I woke up the next morning doubled over in pain. The pressure inside me was so great I could barely stand it. I had to do something, so I downed beer after beer until I became comfortably numb to the pain. Then I drove to class feeling a little tipsy.

The alcohol really helped. I managed to sit through Mr. Zanski's class in only minimal pain and without leaving my body once. But I worried about the lab later that afternoon. The alcohol was beginning to wear off and I didn't want to feel that intense, unbearable pain or leave my body again.

"Hey Pam, it's our last week before finals, so how 'bout I treat you to lunch today at that little Mexican restaurant you like downtown?"

"Sure, thanks, Lily," Pam said.

I really didn't care so much about the food, but it was a good cover to drink, and after three margaritas I had a nice buzz and felt ready to go to the chemistry lab.

Standing in front of my lab bench, I stared at the pretty blue solution in the beaker I had placed over the Bunsen burner, feeling relaxed from the alcohol, wondering what would happen if I suddenly left my body while I was standing up. Would I fall to the ground? Or would I stay standing? I looked over at Mr. Zanski talking to a soft-spoken, smart-looking Asian girl and tried to imagine him naked. He caught me staring at him and smiled, showing off his cute dimples and straight white teeth. Just looking at him made me feel all warm and tingly inside.

"Lily!" Pam nudged me and pointed at my solution, which had bubbled up and was frothing over the sides. "It looks like you might want to turn the Bunsen burner off now."

Mr. Zanski's smile gave me hope that he would approach me, maybe flirt with me or even ask me out. I kept my fingers crossed. But when the bell rang, he gathered his books and walked out the door. He didn't even seem to notice me.

Driving home that day my mind raced with so many questions. *What the hell is wrong with me? Why doesn't Zanski want me? Am I not pretty enough? Smart enough? Good enough? Can't he see what he's doing to me? All the pain and hurt he's causing me? How can he be so cruel? I just want to touch him. Kiss him. Be with him. Why can't he just wrap his arms around me and love me?*

Suddenly, after having been in the class for eleven weeks, it hit me like a ton of bricks. The tall thin body, the piercing brown eyes, the big smile, the carefree laughter, the sarcastic comments, the funny jokes—Mr. Zanski was like a taller, thinner version of my dad. He made me feel just like I'd felt when I was with my dad. It wasn't Zanski's arms I wanted wrapped around me, it was my dad's! Even after everything my dad had done, I still loved him, I still wanted him. I heard my dad's voice calling out to me, "Lil, no one will ever love you more than your da—"

"Fuck!" I screamed as loud as I could, trying to drown out his voice as well as the pain. "I can't do this anymore!" I burst into tears and hit the accelerator, driving full speed ahead toward a parked semi-truck. I intended to slam into the semi and end my life like I should have done before when I'd lived at Rick's. But suddenly an image of me in a wheelchair paralyzed from the neck down flashed across my mind. I saw myself surviving the accident but being left a quadriplegic. "Fuck!" I screamed out loud again. I slammed on my brakes and swerved to the left, narrowly missing the semi, realizing that with my luck that was exactly what would have happened to me. Feeling depressed and alone, I looked forward to my upcoming appointment with Sharyn.

The next day I sat in Sharyn's office and cried, believing I had gone crazy. "I think there's something seriously wrong with me. The other day I was just sitting there in class, and I left my body. I was gone. I couldn't hear or see anything around me. I was trapped in some dark place where all I could hear were my own screams. I was so scared I would never find my way out. So, be honest, Sharyn, am I going crazy?"

"I promise you, Lily, you're not going crazy," she said, calming me down. "You're dissociating, or what feels like disconnecting, from your body. Do you remember when we talked about that before?"

"No, not really. Lately I barely even remember my own name. So who does that? Only crazy people?"

"A soldier in combat, a child being abused, anyone who is experiencing trauma can dissociate in order to protect themselves and survive. But dissociating is not just something trauma survivors do."

"It's not?"

"No, everyone dissociates to varying degrees."

"Everybody? Really?"

"Sure, like when you've arrived at your destination but you can't remember driving there, or getting lost in a really good book."

"I didn't know that! Thanks. I feel a little better knowing I'm not the only one who dissociates."

"Do you remember when you first started feeling like you were going to leave your body?" Sharyn asked.

"Yeah, I was looking at my teacher, Mr. Zanski," I replied. "I don't like to think about it, but he reminds me of my dad."

"Do you ever remember feeling like you wanted to leave your body when you were with your dad?"

"No. Never."

"Well, I know you do not believe your dad was ever inappropriate with you. And you're probably going to get angry with me for saying this, but from what you've told me about your feelings and thoughts about Mr. Zanski, I think this may be stirring up some intense and confusing feelings about your relationship with your dad. What do you think?"

I shrugged and looked down at the floor. Even though what Sharyn was saying made sense, I still didn't think my dad's touching me when I was sixteen was inappropriate or believe he had ever touched me as a child.

"I know that right now you feel like your life is a living hell. And you have every reason to feel that way. But I am so happy that this Mr. Zanski has come into your life, because believe it or not, he is like an angel in disguise."

"Huh? An angel?" I asked, wondering who the crazy one was.

"Yes, an angel. By stirring up some of the intense and confusing feelings about your dad, you can begin the process of looking at these feelings and working through them, and I'm very thankful for that. Sometimes people who come along in our life during a certain time in our healing can trigger our old traumas."

"Oh, Sharyn, I don't remember anything like that. My dad was never inappropriate with me." Sharyn just smiled. Sometimes I wondered if she knew something I didn't.

"You'll remember all that you need to remember when you're ready, Lily, and again, I'm just very thankful for Mr. Zanski."

"Well, I don't feel very thankful at all. Last night I almost ended my life."

"It sounds like you are having a very difficult time dealing with Mr. Zanski."

"Yes, I really am. Sometimes I feel like I can't do this anymore. I can't keep living with all of this pain I feel inside. The only thing I've found to help me feel better is alcohol. At least it numbs the pain."

That day Sharyn and I made some important agreements that probably saved my life. "First, no more alcohol," Sharyn said firmly.

I whined and complained, "But, Sharyn, you don't understand!

It's the only thing that numbs the pain!"

"While it may feel like the alcohol is helping you to feel better, it's not. Trust me. Alcohol is a depressant, which will only make you feel more depressed. And, Lily, I'm sorry, but I can't help you if you come to my office drunk." I really didn't want to give up alcohol, but she offered me another possibility—a referral to someone who could prescribe an antidepressant as a temporary measure to help me with my depression, inability to sleep, and suicidal thoughts. Because I had come to trust her, I agreed.

We also made a pact that day in which I promised I would not commit suicide. I swore I would reach out and call Sharyn immediately if I were struggling and experiencing the need to end my life. In return, Sharyn promised I would get better—she gave me her word.

As I walked to my car after my therapy session, I felt angry at Mr. Zanski. I wished I had never met him and believed that if I hadn't, I would be just fine. I had no idea then what Mr. Zanski had stirred up in me and how important it would be for my recovery. I didn't realize that he truly was my angel in disguise, as Sharyn had wisely pointed out during our session.

Chapter 16
REPRESSED MEMORIES

For the next few months, I continued taking antidepressants and going to my sessions with Sharyn. I was enjoying my classes and working as a waitress at Bob's Big Boy. When we had time, Anthony and I would bowl a few games, catch a concert or movie, or have dinner at a nice restaurant. I was finally starting to feel happy again.

I had always been so sure my dad had never molested me when I was little. Now, I wasn't so sure. I wondered if Sharyn was right about Mr. Zanski stirring up some intense feelings about my dad. Why did I dissociate when Mr. Zanski was near me? Chrissy said Dad had started touching her when she was four. Did Dad touch me when I was four, too? Maybe I'd repressed any memories of molestation. But how could I ever know if my dad had molested me if I couldn't remember anything? Sharyn suggested I ask myself, just before drifting off to sleep, if my dad ever molested me when I was little.

That night before bed I asked myself, "Did my dad ever molest me when I was little?" over and over again until I fell asleep. I dreamt I was being chased by some sort of evil being. I was running and trying to find a place to hide, and just when it was about to catch me, I woke up drenched in sweat. I'd had no dreams or memories of my dad molesting me when I was seven or younger. So for the rest of the week before bed, I didn't bother to ask myself that question again.

The following week, after nearly five years of therapy, Anthony and I were in bed one morning snuggling under the duvet. I pulled Anthony toward my naked body, wiggling my ice-cold toes under his toasty warm legs. He jumped. I giggled. He kissed me. I smiled and kissed him back.

Feeling content, I slowly traced the outline of his nipple with my fingers, watching it pucker. Suddenly it wasn't Anthony's chest I was looking at; it was my dad's. I thought back to when I lay in the cabin in Tahoe with my dad, naked and doing the same exact thing, remembering how happy I had been. Then suddenly, without warning, I had a flashback like nothing I'd ever experienced before. I started to remember pieces of a memory that had been repressed for over twenty-three years.

I was four years old and I didn't know where I was. Everything was gray, hazy, and eerily silent. Through the thick fog I saw Daddy. He was standing there smiling at me with those big brown puppy dog eyes that I loved and trusted so much, melting my heart. I was so happy. I wanted to run to him and jump into his arms. Then the fog suddenly lifted and I saw the chipped sink, the stained toilet, and the big white bathtub. In that instant I knew I was in Daddy's bathroom. I heard the front door open and Daddy whispering, "Shh, remember, Lil, this is our game, our secret," as he hurried me out of the bathroom. At first I couldn't remember what game Daddy was talking about or why I was there. Then the words "Lollipop Game" lit up my whole body on the inside like a big flashing red neon sign, and fragmented pieces of what had happened here came back to me.

I remembered Daddy saying, "I want you to pretend my private part is a lollipop, and I want you to lick it like you are enjoying the biggest, sweetest-tasting lollipop ever, and if you pretend really, really, well, Daddy will get you a real lollipop to enjoy." I was really, really scared. So I did what I always did when I got really, really scared: I left. I squeezed my eyes shut really tightly and before I knew it, my mind traveled to the candy shop, where I sat slowly licking a big slippery, sweet rainbow-swirl lollipop.

Then the fog rolled back in, and everything was gray and hazy again.

Suddenly I was back in the room with Anthony, sweating and shaking all over. I could almost taste my dad's cum spilling into my little mouth, almost feel the urge to gag as I tried to swallow it as fast as I could.

I felt someone shaking me. I looked up. It was Anthony.

"Lil! Lil! What's wrong? Are you okay?" Anthony asked.

"Oh my God, Anthony! No! I'm not okay! I'm scared! All of a sudden I was four again, in my dad's bathroom, and I just knew my dad was about to molest me, and that it had happened before—a lot!" I screamed.

Anthony looked at me with shock as tears ran down my face. "Wait. What? Lil, slow down. What do you mean you just knew?"

"I mean, I *just knew*. I felt it. First, there was a fog that covered everything. Then the fog lifted, I saw my dad in the bathroom, and all these emotions came rushing back. They shot through me like a jolt of electricity, terrorizing me all over again. I just know I was sexually abused by my dad in the bathroom that day, and I know it had happened before. It was all very real."

"Are you sure this really happened and it wasn't just a nightmare?"

"A nightmare? No. I wasn't sleeping. I wasn't dreaming. I was awake, and while I didn't see my dad doing anything to me, I *felt* it. I felt it *all*. And, I *heard* him. He said he wanted me to pretend his private part was a lollipop. He said if I licked it really good he'd buy me a real lollipop. And, somehow, I remembered that sick game. It was the Lollipop Game. So yes, I'm sure. It really happened."

"I want to kill your father," Anthony said angrily.

"Yeah, part of me does too," I said as Anthony wiped my tears. "I mean, it's not the same as when I was sixteen, feeling all grown-up and wanting to have sex, thinking what my dad and I had was real love. I was just a helpless, terrified little girl who just wanted to be loved by her dad. Loved, not molested!" I sobbed as I buried my face in Anthony's chest, remembering how my brave inner child Lil had hated her body so much that she tried hiding it under all that fur. She wished her daddy would stop touching her. Lil believed that if the parts of her body that brought this icky sort of unwanted attention were so well hidden under fur that Daddy couldn't find them, her wish would finally come true.

During our next session, Sharyn reassured me that what I had experienced was completely normal. In order to block out what was too horrific for me to deal with when I was four, I had repressed the memory—until now. The good news was that I was now strong enough to handle what I couldn't before. I was healing.

"And how do you know I'm strong enough now? I don't feel strong at all. I'm barely surviving. I feel anxious and shaky. It's like I'm right on the edge of a cliff. How do you know another flashback won't send me over the edge?" I asked as I reached for another tissue, still in shock that my dad had really molested me. I felt dirty and used.

"Because, Lily, your mind is your protector. It wants you to survive, and it will *never* reveal any repressed memory before you're ready, before you're strong enough to handle it."

I must have been stronger than I thought, because the next day I flashed back to one late summer evening when I was five.

After an exhausting day at Disneyland, Daddy and I were spending the night on a friend's living room floor, our sleeping bags touching. Daddy was slowly unzipping my sleeping bag. Scared, I gazed through the front window and concentrated really, really hard on the dimly lit front yard, and then, before Daddy's hand could touch me, I left my body like a Disney character stepping out of her costume, and went outside to play.

It scared me how I could remember very vividly every parked car, every street light, every blade of grass once I'd dissociated, but I couldn't remember one thing that had happened in the living room. Sharyn said that when someone dissociates, it's common and normal to remember things in the way that I did, and that made me feel a little better.

My next flashback happened about a month later as I was getting ready for bed. I suddenly recalled a third repressed memory.

I was six years old. Daddy and I were driving in his pretty blue Chevy station wagon when he said in his strange, sexy voice, "Come here, Lil."

I somehow already knew what would happen when I heard that voice, so I angrily responded, "No! I don't want to!"

He replied soothingly, "Oh, Lily, come on now. You know this is just how daddies show that they love their special daughters. So, come here, come on." Not really wanting to, I slowly moved toward him as he gently guided me over the shiny blue bench seat, resting me on his lap. "Remember, Lil, no one else in the whole wide world will ever love you more than your Daddy," Daddy said as he reached between my legs.

I gazed out the window and suddenly, in some far-away

corner of my mind, I was snuggled up under Pegasus's wing all safe and warm. It was my safe place I liked to go when I was really scared, a place where not even Daddy could touch me.

I had dissociated again. Dissociating always saved me when things got too scary and overwhelming for me to handle. It was the only way I had to escape. As I remembered and relived how I had felt then, I cried for that very sad little girl who'd had to leave her body in order to survive the abuse.

A few months later I was lying on my bed, books and papers scattered all around me, studying for an organic chemistry test. I had recently transferred to San Jose State University, so happy that my chemistry teacher was no longer Mr. Zanski. One minute I was reading my textbook, wondering if I would ever understand the synthesis of substituted benzenes, and then the next minute, I uncovered another repressed memory. Suddenly I was five years old again, a good little girl who believed in two things—her daddy and fairy tales.

I lay snuggled up in my bed as Daddy read Cinderella. "Lil, can you keep a secret?" I eagerly nodded my head. "Do you know who the prince really is?" I stared at him wide-eyed and shook my head. He smiled and said, "He's really Cinderella's father." I looked at him shocked. "Shh, now remember, Lil, please don't tell anyone. It's a secret," he whispered, and I crossed my heart and swore never to tell. "You see, Lil, even Cinderella knows no one else in the whole kingdom will love her more than her daddy," he said. He leaned over and lifted my nightgown. Before his hand could touch my pink lace undies, I left my body and disappeared into the pages of my Cinderella book, wondering how she felt when she finally found out who her prince charming really *was.*

As I sat on my bed crying, I suddenly realized my father had invaded and violated not only my body, but also my mind. Not even my imaginary world or beloved fairy tales were safe, and there was something about that which seemed so sick and abominable. In some ways it felt even worse to me than the sexual abuse.

Two months later, I had another flashback. I was seven years old, a frightened little girl who couldn't understand why her mommy was taking her to see a therapist when the only person she really wanted to see was her daddy.

The next morning I called my mom. "Mom, I'm starting to remember things about when I was little. So why did you take me to a therapist when I was seven anyway?" Normally we didn't talk about the past, but I wanted to know.

"Well, Lily, I took you because I thought your father was molesting you, but you'd never talk to me about it, so I thought you might open up and talk about it with a therapist." I didn't tell her I remembered being molested. I didn't like talking about my dad with my mom.

"So what happened?"

"The therapist was convinced you were being sexually abused and said he would testify in court that your father was molesting you. I told your father he could never come near you again, and if he didn't sign the papers giving up his parental rights so you could be adopted by Jeffrey, I'd press charges against him."

I finally understood why my dad had left me when I was seven. He didn't want to go to jail. How ironic it was that my dad was sitting in jail right now.

As painful as it was, it did feel really good to finally be strong enough to remember what my mind had kept from me all these years. But knowing the truth left me feeling shattered. I was suddenly being forced to fit together pieces of an ugly puzzle I didn't want to put together. But I knew I needed to; I didn't want to feel broken anymore. So, over the next two years, I worked really hard with Sharyn to put all those pieces back together again as best I could. I never did remember the sexual abuse that happened once I'd dissociated, and thankfully I never needed to. For me, just knowing my dad had molested me was enough. During those two years, without even being aware of it, I was healing and becoming whole again.

During that time, I joined my first women's group for survivors of child sexual abuse, the Healing Steps workshop, run by Sharyn. (For more information about the healing steps, check out Sharyn Higdon Jones's *Healing Steps* Workbook.) I had never heard another woman speak about her abuse before. Sitting in a circle, I listened as one woman began telling her story of being molested—*once*. She was ten years old when it happened. The experience had left her totally devastated. As I looked around the circle, everyone seemed to be very sad for her. I wasn't. I thought, *Lady, you were molested only* once. *Get over it already. That's not devastating.* In comparison, my story was far worse. I couldn't count how many times I'd been molested by Carlos or even guess at the extent of the abuse inflicted by my father. Besides, if she really wanted to know what it felt like to be totally devastated, she should try throwing her dad, who was once her lover, in prison. But as I sat there impatiently waiting for her to finish her story so that I could tell mine, I heard her cry of pain, a cry I knew all too well. At that moment I realized it didn't matter if she had been molested once or a thousand times, her little girl's pain was no different from mine. We had both gone to that same dark and lonely place where no child should ever have to go. In fact, as we went around the circle and shared our stories, each one as unique as our fingerprints, every cry of pain I heard sounded exactly the same, and I knew we had all gone there. We all knew how it felt to be abused and broken. I felt a real connection with each brave and beautiful woman sitting in the circle with me. They felt like my sisters. I felt like I was home.

Chapter 17
ENDING THE CYCLE OF ABUSE

For as long as I could remember, there had been a knot in my stomach. Sometimes it was small and I barely noticed it, and other times it grew very large and tight. If the knot expanded too much or got too tight, I would get sick. I had gotten so used to the knot that at times I'd forget it was even there.

Inside, tangled in that knot, I could almost feel a raging bull fighting to get free when I got angry. My worst fear was that if I had a baby I would kill it. I was afraid there would come a day when my baby would cry and cry, and I couldn't stop it. Listening to the constant crying, I would get so frustrated and angry that my inner bull would finally burst right out of me and attack the baby to shut it up. I worried I'd have no control over my anger and my baby would have little chance of surviving. I'd be left completely devastated and hating myself for what I had done. So I thought the best thing I could do was never have a baby.

But, in the winter of 1991 an extraordinary thing happened. After seven years and countless hours of therapy, I felt the knot deep within my gut suddenly dissolve, and the raging bull, no longer tangled up in there, went away too. I never realized all the energy I had expended to keep that rage alive within me until it was completely gone, and now I had a place that I could fill with anything I chose.

With the fear and anger gone, I felt so free, so open to possibilities. For the first time in my life, I wanted to have a baby—a child I could love unconditionally the way I wished I had been loved when I was a child. More than anything, I wanted to be the parent I always wished I'd had.

Once the knot had dissolved I stopped taking my antidepressants. After having been on them for about two and a half years, I knew that I didn't need them anymore. I also knew I didn't need to see Sharyn on a weekly basis anymore. I thanked her for all the help and guidance she had given me during the seven years I'd been seeing her. I told her how grateful I was to have had her as my therapist, that she was like my mom, teacher, and best friend all rolled up into one. Smiling, Sharyn reminded me of how far I'd come and told me that if at anytime I ever needed to talk, she would always be there for me. As our last session came to an end, we hugged, and she told me how proud she was of me and that I was one of the bravest women she knew. She thought I should write a book to help give me a sense of closure and to give other abuse survivors hope. I laughed, not ready then to write a book, but promised that if I ever did, I would never forget that she was the first person to have suggested it.

In May 1992, I graduated with honors from San Jose State University with a B.S. in Chemistry. Life was good. I had put the past behind me and was enjoying living a normal life. It was nice to be free of all the pain and anger and flashbacks.

Anthony and I couldn't have been any happier. We liked spending time together, playing together; heck, we even liked working on home remodeling projects together. Mom and I were getting along too. I felt calm and good inside like I imagined a normal person would. I felt healed.

———

On December 16, 1992, I got a call from Connor. He said Dad had died earlier that day of a massive heart attack. Shocked, I just stood there. I couldn't believe my dad was dead. I mean he was really dead, really gone. It had been a long time since I'd thought about my dad. I had thought that when my dad died I would be happy, that I'd celebrate and throw a big party because I knew the world would be a better, safer place without him here molesting children and destroying lives. Instead, I did what I had promised myself I would never do—I cried. No matter how hard I tried to fight it, a part of me still missed my dad and was sad that he had died.

I didn't go to my dad's funeral. Since my dad knew better than anyone how I felt about funerals, I knew he would understand.

The day of my dad's funeral I found out I was pregnant. It was almost as if now that my dad was gone, my body felt safe enough to have a baby.

No one could believe I was pregnant. I had never liked babies. I had always said I would never have a baby and would question the sanity of anyone who did. I would cringe in horror at the mere thought of having a smelly, messy, noisy, spitting-up creepy crawling machine of my very own. And yet, here I was, expecting a baby and thrilled.

On September 11, 1993, my daughter Amy was born, and my life was forever changed. The doctor welcomed my crying newborn daughter into the world and then placed her upon my chest. Exhausted but curious, I looked down and watched as she took hold of my light blue hospital gown and then fell back asleep, soothed by my familiar heartbeat. In an instant I fell madly in love.

Amy weighed eight pounds, six ounces, and had big, brown, gentle eyes with very long eyelashes like those of a newborn fawn. I would rock her while closely examining her perfect little fingers and her perfect little toes, thinking to myself that she was the most perfect thing I had ever seen. I was sure that with all the love I had for my perfect little girl, I would be a perfect parent. After all, how hard could parenting be? Well, I would soon find out when reality slapped me in the face, and it hurt.

Over the next few years I tried hard to make Amy happy, but she was very different from me. She didn't like the beach, the park, or even other kids. I was frustrated that Amy would rather be home alone with a book or puzzle than be outside playing. It worried me because I thought she should want to socialize. I thought Amy would surely love to ride a bike just like I used to love riding my Breeze, but when the training wheels came off and she took her first fall, she refused to get back on her bike. As she screamed, "I hate bike riding! Bikes hurt!" and then refused to go anywhere near her bike, alarm bells went off in my head. I remembered reading somewhere that when you fall, you had to get right back up and try again. What sort of parent would I be if I allowed my daughter to just walk away? Part of me wanted to hit her, to save her from herself, especially since I felt it was for her own good, but the other part of me just couldn't do it. I remembered how it felt to be hit. Even though I was frustrated, I did not repeat the cycle of physical abuse.

Although I'd vowed to be the best parent I could be, I quickly found I had a void within me on how to be that parent. I had no examples of what a good parent is. My mom had taught me how to live in constant fear of her yelling and beatings in an attempt to force me to behave. I knew this did not work because I had learned nothing except how to run to escape the violence and pain. My dad had taught me that one's own needs and wants come first, always. Things like trust and love were to be used and exploited in order to satisfy one's own desires. I'd learned what it felt like to be used and to feel worthless and stupid. He'd left me completely broken. I knew all too well how devastating this type of parenting was, and I had no interest in being this sort of parent either.

To fill that void, I read parenting books and went to parenting classes, support groups, and seminars. But no matter how hard I tried, I still felt disconnected from Amy. I didn't understand her. I began to grow even more frustrated, and I noticed that as my frustration grew, so did my anger. I felt like a failure as a parent.

I finally found a book that changed my life and my ability to be a good parent. It was *The Enneagram of Parenting* by Elizabeth Wagele. The Enneagram allowed me to see the world through Amy's eyes. I finally realized that Amy was not a sad loner but a curious introvert, a Five-Observer personality type, who just wants to understand everything. She was my little Miss Einstein, and once I understood her, she became a happier child and I became a better parent, which allowed our mother-daughter relationship to flourish and grow. When I discovered that I was a Two-Helper personality type who just wants to be of assistance and to be liked, I realized that Amy felt just as frustrated with me as I did with her. As a Five-Observer, Amy had a built-in difficulty with me, the Two-Helper Mom, because she viewed my helping as intruding into her business, and for her there was nothing worse. Once I read this book and my perspective shifted, so many frustrations and misunderstandings ceased to be. I not only learned a lot about Amy, but I also learned a lot about myself.

I learned that what had hurt me as a child far more deeply than any abuse I had ever suffered was not being loved unconditionally by my parents. I'd felt that I would rather die than live in a world where I was not loved, which helped me to understand why I had clung so tightly to my dad as a teen. When I read that the basic desire of a Two, me, was to be loved unconditionally, I felt enormous relief. I was finally able to see myself more clearly.

———

Everything continued along smoothly until Amy reached fifth grade, when she began to lie to Anthony and me about her homework. As I sat on the couch in the living room wondering whether or not it was normal for a child to lie, the phone rang. "Hello, Lily," said Mom. We talked at least once a week, if not more.

"Hi Mom," I said.

"So, how's Amy?" Mom asked. She always wanted to know how her granddaughter was doing.

"Well, I'm having a problem with her lying," I said. I didn't usually talk to my mom about parenting, but she'd caught me at a weak moment.

"What do you mean?" Mom asked in a concerned voice.

"Oh, she's been leaving her homework at school and then not doing it. So, today I asked her if she had her homework in her backpack and she looked right at me and said 'Yes.' She promised me that she had it. But when we got home, she didn't. She lied right to my face, Mom," I said as tears rolled down my cheeks. I felt so hurt that my daughter would or could do that.

"Do you remember how you always said that you never, ever wanted to hit your child like your siblings hit their children? Do you remember saying that?" Mom asked excitedly. Mom didn't like to talk about the past and how she had hit me and my siblings, but she was quick to discuss how it was okay for my siblings to hit their own children.

"Yes, I did say that, and I meant it, too. I don't ever want to hit Amy," I replied. I stood by that. I'd made a vow to myself and to my daughter that I would never hit her like my mom had hit me. I had broken the cycle of abuse.

"Well, Lily," Mom laughed with her knowing voice, "if you'd been hitting Amy, she wouldn't be lying to you right now." Mom's words turned my stomach, stopped my tears, and reminded me why I didn't discuss parenting with her. That night Anthony and I talked with Amy about her lying and found out that she wasn't bringing her homework home because it was too hard. She was struggling. So, we got her the help she needed, and from that point on, Amy has excelled in school.

The last time I saw my mom was when Amy was in sixth grade. Mom was down for a visit. One afternoon, Mom and I jumped into my white Jeep Cherokee and headed over to pick Amy up from school.

"Hi, Nana," Amy said excitedly as she climbed in the back seat and motioned Nana to come sit next to her.

"Hi, Amy, how was school?" Mom asked as she got comfortable in the back seat next to Amy.

"Okay," Amy replied shyly. Mom gently tickled Amy, getting her to loosen up and smile.

"You know, Amy, I think you're old enough now to know the truth, and it's time for your Nana to tell you," Mom said. Amy looked at Mom, ready to know whatever it was my mom wanted to tell her. As I drove, I kept one eye on Mom in the rearview mirror. She had a smug look on her face. I had no idea what she was talking about, but I was curious to find out.

"Tell me what, Nana?" Amy asked, eager to know. I was eager to know too.

"I wanted to tell you about two girls who were camping at Yosemite last week. That's where you'll be going with your class next month, right?" Mom asked.

"Yes," Amy replied. She was looking forward to the week long, sixth grade field trip.

"Well, one night, while the two girls were fast asleep, a bear got into their tent. One girl was on her period and the other wasn't. You'll never guess what happened next."

"What, Nana?" Amy asked, wide-eyed and concerned.

"The bear smelled the blood of the girl on her period and ate her alive. This is why no girl should ever go camping when she's on her period. I think you're old enough now to know that," my mom said, smiling, delighted to be the one to share this important information with her granddaughter.

"Mom! Stop! What are you talking about? That's not true." I looked into the rearview mirror and saw my daughter's face overcome with terror as she listened to my mom's "truth," the "truth" that she had been so eager to share. At that moment, I was transported back to my childhood, when I had felt the same exact terror that was now written across my daughter's face.

"Oh, Lily, of course it's true," my mom said confidently, sounding surprised by my comment. "Don't you read the newspaper?" The truth was I didn't read the newspaper, so I wasn't one hundred percent certain if it was true or not. What I did know to be true was that I had recently shared with my mom that Amy had just started her period, and that she was very self-conscious about it. So, why in the world would my mom share something like that, true or not, knowing what I had told her?

Mom had crossed the boundary. I was never going to let anyone hurt Amy, and that included my mom. I would not allow Mom's fear to permeate my daughter's safe and healthy world, which I had worked so hard to create. I had come too far. I had to choose, and I chose Amy.

Once Mom left to go back to Pocatello, Amy and I sat down at the computer, and together we learned all about bears. Afterward, I quizzed Amy on her newfound bear facts.

"Amy, how many people have been killed by bears in Yosemite?" I asked.

"Zero," Amy stated confidently.

"Correct. When might a bear hurt you?" I asked.

"When he's hungry and you have food," Amy said knowingly. Next, we discussed the park's policies and the use of airtight containers for all food items.

"Do bears in Yosemite care about the smell of blood?" I asked.

"No," Amy said.

"Which bear does show a tiny amount of interest in blood?" I asked.

"Polar bears," Amy replied.

"Yes. And do polar bears live in Yosemite?" I asked.

"No," Amy laughed, and I laughed too. We hugged, and Amy felt much better.

"Mommy, if that stuff about bears killing people in Yosemite isn't true, then why did Nana say it was?" Amy asked, confused.

"I don't know, Amy. I just don't know," I sadly replied, slowly shaking my head.

Amy had a blast in Yosemite. She and her classmates never did come across any bears.

I explained to my mom that I felt she had crossed the line with her fearful bear tale. She didn't understand. I let my mom know that I loved her very much, but we would not be getting together anymore, and she would no longer see her granddaughter. I haven't seen my mom since. Although we do not see each other or talk, I do send my mom flowers twice a year—on her birthday and Christmas. Actually, I know my mom has an inner child too, and I'm really sending them to her. I feel bad for her, and even though I can't rescue her (only my mom can do that for herself), I can send her pretty fresh flowers and hope they make her smile. Mom is doing well in Pocatello and has recently married her eighth husband.

Chapter 18
CONCLUSION

I went to lunch with one of the women from the Healing Steps workshop. She asked, "Lily, how did you overcome a childhood of horrors?"

"It's simple really," I said. "I had to. If I hadn't, I wouldn't still be here. I would be just another suicide statistic."

I've never blamed my parents for the abuse. They were just doing to me what had been done to them, doing the best they could with the limited tools they had. But I did get angry that *they* couldn't see that. Instead they chose to remain victims and then perpetrators. They refused to take responsibility for their actions, refused to do something—*anything*—to stop the cycles of abuse.

I knew I'd never be happy doing what had been done to me, continuing the cycles that had left me broken. Although at first I had no idea how to break the cycles, or if it were even possible, I had to try. I had to know if I could rid myself of the patterns of abuse deeply ingrained in me. And once I knew that it was possible for me to break the cycles, that I didn't have to repeat the abuse and ruin my life and the lives of others, I didn't stop trying until I succeeded.

Anthony thinks it's funny that before we got married I had told him, "Hey, don't expect me to stay married to you for more than five years, okay? Because that's the longest my mom has ever been married and I don't think I know how to do this marriage thing any differently. Besides, I'm just doing this so we can get to the fun part, the honeymoon." I knew that after our wedding in Pocatello, we were flying to Maui, and I couldn't wait.

"Okay, Lil, that's fine," Anthony replied. "I'll take the five years being married to you, but I can picture us growing old together. I know we'll be happily married for our entire lives, just like my parents," to which I laughed hysterically.

"Yeah, you don't know much, do you?" I responded, trying to stop my uncontrollable laughter.

Yet here I am, married over thirty years now, and I finally understand what an amazing relationship Anthony and I have, a true love people search for their whole lives. My husband is my best friend and my lover. Through the good times and the bad he's always been right there with me, ready to catch me if I fall. Somehow he always knows when I need a hug or some reassurance that everything is going to be okay. After all these years, we are still madly in love, and we still love to have fun and play together. Sometimes we fight, and then make up, but I think making up is the best part. Looking back, I guess I was the crazy one who didn't believe in us or in living happily ever after. Now I believe. I'm so lucky to have found my *real* Prince Charming.

Besides being married to the most wonderful man in the world, I also have the most wonderful daughter. Today Amy is a senior in college, an honor student majoring in mechanical engineering. She is a self-confident and passionate young lady who knows without any doubt that her dad and I love and support her unconditionally— always and forever, no matter what. And even though she may not fully understand the significance and greatness of the fact that she *is* the child with whom all cycles of abuse—physical, emotional, and sexual—have finally been broken, I do. And by breaking the cycles of abuse, I have forever changed the legacies of future generations. It still brings tears to my eyes when I think about how my wish came true. I am the parent I always wished I'd had.

I can only hope the cycles of abuse have been broken in my siblings' families. Eileen has been married four times, and Cindy has been married three times. Eileen, Cindy, and Bart all have used spanking or hitting to discipline their children. I hope they were able to keep their anger in check better than our mom did and never let their spankings lead to physical abuse. I also hope they were able to keep their yelling from escalating to emotional abuse. In the heat of the moment it seems like a very easy line to cross.

Although Connor wasn't abused, he was neglected. I read that when children are victims of neglect, they are more likely to abuse drugs or alcohol. Feeling unwanted and worthless, Connor turned to marijuana to ease his pain, and he continued to smoke dope, often daily, even after he became a parent. His priority was his weed, and that took precedence over everything else, including his kids. As I look at Connor's twenty-year-old daughter's mug shot online (this time she was arrested for possession of nearly four pounds of marijuana, her face barely recognizable as the happy little girl I once knew), I have to wonder if she feels unwanted and worthless too. A mother herself now, I can only hope she will not let the cycle of neglect continue.

After Dad died, Chrissy and I started talking again. She told me that after Dad was released from prison the second time in the summer of '89, he moved to Arizona, sharing a home with Chrissy, her husband, and their one-year-old son. Chrissy's allowing Dad to move in with her gave him access to her son—setting her son up to be molested (the Molest Cycle). Chrissy felt she could always protect her son from our dad's sexual advances. In fact, she insisted that she did. And she insisted that Dad had changed and didn't touch kids anymore. For her son's sake, and for the sake of every child my dad came in contact with while staying with her, I hope that's true.

Sometimes, I miss my dad. Normally, I would turn to my sweet and supportive husband Anthony for comfort, but he holds a hate in his heart toward my father, toward any father who would do something so despicable as molest his own daughter. I understand his hate, I understand the world's hate, but sometimes I get tired of understanding. Sometimes, I wish someone would understand me.

I call the one person who does, my sister Chrissy.

One cold and dark winter evening, a few years after Dad died, I called Chrissy. "Do you miss Dad sometimes?" I asked for the first time.

"Yeah," she answered. She had no idea how much her response meant to me. Then she talked about her frustration with the people around her who learned our dad was a child molester and proceeded to attack him with the hate of the world. She felt that no one else in the world understood her feelings. I do. I love you, Chrissy.

Over the years I have found that you can forgive the person without excusing the act. Letting go of the anger makes way for compassion, kindness, and peace. I found such compassion and understanding through an empowering dream I experienced in the summer of 2010. This dream would forever change the way I viewed my dad.

I was a little girl playing at the beach, bucket and shovel in hand. I happened to meet the sweetest little boy—his name was Billy. He shared with me that his biggest wish and greatest dream was to grow up to be a famous man possessing the extraordinary gift of superhuman power and strength to fight the evils of the world—an honest-to-goodness superhero—someone everyone admired and turned to in times of trouble. He hungered to undertake tasks that no one else would dare attempt, to be the big hero. Ah, the fortune, the fame, the glory—he fantasized about it all. It meant the world to him and he just couldn't wait; he was such an impatient boy.

We played together in the sand—me building the sandcastles and him creating the larger-than-life people and creatures. We laughed and giggled as we made up stories to go with our sand creations—stories of long, perilous journeys to far off underworlds in the sand, which tested Billy's endurance, courage, and cunning. We imagined people needing to be saved from relentlessly ruthless villains, and only SuperBilly could save the day—just in the nick of time too—before the bad guys totally destroyed their beloved sand world. I heard the waves calling me, so I went to chase them as they lapped onto the beach, while Billy stayed behind to add some finishing touches to his latest sand creation.

I was having a wonderfully splendid time dancing in the waves, busily pursuing the sand crabs as they dug swiftly into the wet sand, with me digging madly right behind. Suddenly, I heard screams of terror and turned to see my buddy's dad kicking and beating him senselessly—each blow violently sending him crashing into our sand creations, completely demolishing them. Then, as Billy lay motionless in the sand, his father proceeded to brutally rape him.

I wept as I saw Billy being beaten and raped—I watched helplessly as all his dreams crumbled just like our sand world. I saw a terrified, destroyed little boy, a boy who dreamt of superpowers and bigness, but now was powerless and small as he melted into the sand, and beach and boy became one. He had no place to hide—his grandiose illusions of bigness and superhero power had been swept out to sea. As Billy lifted his face covered with a mixture of tears, blood, and sand, our eyes made contact for a split second and his intense sadness was my sadness too. I understood exactly how he felt—weak, defenseless, small, insignificant, worthless, alone, and lost.

Humiliated and completely broken beyond repair, Billy hesitantly got up, brushed himself off, mustered up all his courage and strength, and began to run faster and faster away from me, his father, and our once magnificent sand creations. Instead of getting smaller and smaller in size as he got farther and farther away, he grew bigger and bigger until he had grown to the size of a real adult, right in front of my eyes. I got the sense that he was ashamed and wanted to hide from *me, his father, and the world, so that no one would know his pain or his identity. He had finally gotten at least part of his wish—to become a big person—and as he turned his head for just a split second, I caught a glimpse of his face. Oh my God—Billy was my dad! The physical, outer shell was my dad, but I had peered beyond the shell and still saw the little boy within.*

Sadly, my dad never did get his wish of being a superhero with great super powers, which totally crushed him. Sadder still, he found that he felt big and powerful only when he inflicted the same degree of pain and torment that he had experienced on others smaller than himself. He believed this to be his only option—to recreate what he felt deep within his soul, inflicting on others the same abuse he'd endured on the beach that day at the hands of his father, the day his dreams died.

This dream made me realize that I had to choose to forgive the little boy who lived within my dad, the little boy who believed he had no choice but to suffer in silence. I also had to choose to forgive the man he grew up to be. If I didn't, I would never be set free. Once I did, I felt nothing but the tenderest pity and sorrow for my dad.

Dad and I aren't really all that different. We were both abused. But I chose to face the scary inner demons lurking deep within me. Dad didn't. The little boy had lived within my dad in some dark and lonely place, buried under the pain, the hurt, the anger, and the rage just like my inner child Lil had. My dad lashed out as I had when I beat those sweet little kittens because he wanted to be the perpetrator, not the victim. I wish my dad could have known how much little Billy desperately needed to be rescued and loved by him. Had my dad been strong enough and had the help to do that, I think Billy could have been the big hero he had always hungered to be.

I know my dad is now in Angel Land, surrounded by the softest angel wings, which shimmer in a bright white and pink glow, a land I'd caught a glimpse of once in my dream. He didn't want me to go there when I was seven, but at fifty-four, he was ready to go. I know one day I'll go there too. I hear that everything you wish for is granted up in Angel Land, so on my dad's birthday, April 1, when others around me are busy playing tricks and jokes on their dear ones, when laughter, silliness, and happiness is everywhere, I look up and see my daddy high in the clouds being SuperBilly, saving the day in his new land. And I let him know that if he comes across some really, really bad guys, to picture me, his bravest Lil, fighting right alongside him, because we both know that those bad guys don't stand a chance!

AFTERWORD

I decided to write this book for two reasons. First, I promised my inner child I'd tell her story—a story I knew but didn't yet understand. My father had done unspeakable things to me when I was little—some would say unforgivable things—but he'd also rescued me from my abusive mother who scared me to death, and he'd saved me when I lay dying.

At first I had no idea how to tell my inner child's story. But then I had a dream. It was about my father, forgiveness, and me. That dream is where I began writing my book—the end written first. Seven years later I finished writing my final version of my book, but I never changed that perfect ending. I know it sounds crazy, but for all she's been through and for all she's taught me, my inner child is my hero.

The second reason I wrote this book is that I truly believe my experience of survival, healing, and breaking the cycles of abuse will provide hope and ultimately help people. There have been many memoirs that explore the issues of child abuse and suffering, but they neglect to describe the healing process. Instead, most memoirs conclude with the end of the abuse. To me, when the abuse ends is when the real story begins. The first part of my book tells the abuse, but the second part details the healing. I believe my memoir offers a message of hope for survivors that sadly cannot be found among most child abuse memoirs.

So, I made it my mission to get my story out there. The process was a long one. I began writing my manuscript in 2010 and sent out my first proposal in 2011. I worked tirelessly over the next five years making various changes and sending my manuscript to hundreds of agents. When nothing panned out, I changed course and began querying small publishing houses. This arduous and sometimes disheartening process continued for another two years until I decided that rather than give up, I would self-publish. I truly believe my book is important, and I made the firm decision that I would never give up on making my story available to help others.

When I began writing this book, I thought I could simply revisit my past from a safe distance. I didn't realize that in order to write my story, I had to relive it. My anxiety increased the more I wrote. A year into my writing I had my first full-blown panic attack while driving. My head pounded, my heart raced, and my sweaty hands trembled wildly. I held on to the steering wheel for dear life as I began to leave my body and dissociate like I had when I was young—a gift then but definitely not now. My greatest fear was that I'd die in a car crash or kill someone because I had left my body, unable to see where I was driving. To be able to drive safely, I was prescribed anti-anxiety medication. While writing this book, I also became depressed, was prescribed antidepressants, and returned to therapy. Without question, telling my story and breaking the silence was far more difficult than I could have possibly imagined. But I did it, and I'm glad I did.

Memoirist and poet Maya Angelou once said, "As soon as healing takes place, go out and heal somebody else." My greatest wish is that *My Daddy the Pedophile* will offer others hope, encouragement, and the knowledge that although the road may be bumpy and the journey long, it is always possible to prevail over great trauma.

ACKNOWLEDGMENTS

I'd like to thank my editor and friend, Alyssa Delaney, for her incredible and tireless editing, her insightful and spot-on suggestions with splashes of humor and funny notes sprinkled in, her unbelievable patience and kindness, and her caring so deeply. I cannot thank her enough for her unwavering support and friendship.

I'd also like to thank my writing coach, Adair Lara, for reading my first draft, as rough as it was, and seeing its potential, for helping me with my invaluable story arc—just knowing the perfect place to begin my story made me believe I could really do this—and for giving me her super helpful and hilarious book on writing memoirs, *Naked, Drunk, and Writing*, which I referred to often while writing my own memoir.

I have great gratitude for Marie L. Bratton for helping me get my first draft out of my head and onto paper and for never letting me forget what a big feat it is for a dyslexic person like me to take on the challenge of writing a memoir.

A very special thanks goes out to my Parents United counselor, Art, for helping me see who my dad really was and for giving me hope when I had none.

I can never adequately thank my therapist, Sharyn Higdon Jones, for helping me put the pieces back together when I was ready to give up. I am so happy to be able to share some of our important therapy work in this book.

I'm very grateful to my daughter for being my perfect reminder why all the work I did to heal was worth it and for all her patience and understanding while I wrote my memoir.

Finally, I want to thank my husband for standing by me when no one else did and for believing that what I have to say is important. Your undying love, support, and encouragement mean more to me than you will ever know.

ABOUT THE AUTHOR

Lily Palazzi lives in northern California with her husband, daughter, and house bunny Shadow. A survivor of incest, abuse and pedophilia, she takes great pride in having broken all cycles of abuse and continues her lifelong healing process by participating in various support groups and workshops for abuse survivors. She brings joy to sick children by serving as a Wish Grantor for the Make-A-Wish Foundation. Her own greatest wish is that her memoir *My Daddy the Pedophile* will offer hope and encouragement to anyone facing difficult times.